be your own spin doctor

A Practical Guide to Using the Media

Paul Richards

TAKE THAT LTD.

Take That Ltd.
P.O.Box 200
Harrogate
HG1 2YR

Fax: +44-1423-526035

sales@takethat.co.uk
www.takethat.co.uk

Text Copyright © 1998 Paul Richards
Design © 1998 Take That Ltd.

10 9 8 7 6 5 4 3 2 1

Printed and bound in Great Britain.

ISBN 1-873668-52-X

'The British Press is a whore
– but occasionally we must get into bed with it.'

Aneurin Bevan MP
(Sign above Peter Mandelson's desk,
Labour Party HQ, Walworth Road, late 1980's).

'We should put the spin doctors in the spin clinics, where
they can meet other spin patients and be treated by spin
consultants. Then the rest of us can get on with the proper
democratic process.'

Tony Benn MP
October 1997

'The world would be a better place without spin doctors'

Bernard Ingham,
PR Week, March 1998

Ackowledgements

Many people helped me in writing this book. The invaluable contribution of some must remain anonymous, but I would like to particularly thank everyone at Take That Ltd, my publisher Chris Brown, Jeremy Baker, Simon Buckby, Tony Brown, Ian Corfield, Lorraine Eames, Derek Draper, Quentin Langley, Tim Lusher, Dermot Kehoe, James Neighbour, Mike Parkinson, Sally Shalam, Bene't Steinberg, Mish Tullar, Ruth Turner, and Benjamin Wegg-Prosser.

Thanks to Denis MacShane for the original inspiration, and to my colleagues at Chelgate, particularly the chairman Terence Fane-Saunders who gave me a great deal of support and excellent advice.

Many of the examples in this book of successful spin doctoring are drawn from the 1997 General Election, and I would like to pay tribute to everyone involved in that historic Labour campaign, from the strategists in Millbank, to the activists who helped me in Billericay.

Finally, thanks to Stella Creasy who almost did the typing.

PAUL RICHARDS
Hammersmith,
London 1998

Editorial Note

'Spin doctor' is a relatively new expression, and as far as I have been able to discover, there is no agreement as to whether it should be hyphenated (spin-doctor) or not. Both forms seem to be used in books and newspapers, so I have chosen to use 'spin doctor' throughout.

Table of Contents

1. Living in Spin   7

The Age Of The Spin Doctor; Your Reputation Matters; Let he that is without spin cast the first stone; A media obsession.

2. Here Is The News   18

What is News?; Who are the Media?; A Love-hate Relationship; Print; Broadcast; News Agencies; Different Types of Journalist.

3. Dealing With The Media   39

Getting it Right; Getting it Wrong; Journalists can be devious too.

4. Planning And Preparation   54

Making a Plan; Context; Message; Staying On-Message; Types of Media; Methods to Employ; When to do it, How Much Will It Cost?; How Do I know if I've Been Successful?; Contacts – Spin Doctoring is a Contact Sport.

5. Spinning In Print   64

News Release
Format; Style and Structure; News Releases must contain News; The Five Ws; Clearing News Releases; A Means Not an End; News Release Checklist.

Features
Opportunities for spin doctors; Doing it your Yourself; Structure and Style; Selling in the Article; Features Checklist.

Other Types of Article
Book Reviews; Obituaries; Profiles; The Life in a Day; My favourite.

Letters to the Editor
Take aim...; ...Fire; Letter Writing Checklist.

Dear Diary

Mind Your Language
Steer Clear of Clichés; Jargon and Acronyms; Get It Right.

6. Spinning On The Air   90

Giving Interviews; Fielding the Bid; Appearance; Body Language; Preparation; Ignore the Question; Constructing Your Soundbite; Avoiding the Chop; Beware the Pitfalls; Following Up; Do's and Don'ts; Radio and Television Phone-ins.

7. Other Ways Of Spinning   102

News Conferences; News Conferences Checklist; Stunts; Stunts checklist; Photo-Opportunities; Photo-opps Checklist; Using A Photographer; Using a photographer Checklist; Spinning On The Net

8. Advanced Spinning   115

Dealing With A Crisis; Rapid Rebuttal; Making Complaints; Complaints Checklist; Spin Doctoring And The Law; The Really Dirty Stuff; Leaks; Briefing against your Enemies; Misinformation; Turning the Rumour Mill; Bribery

Conclusion   133

Appendix One: Spot The Spin   134

Appendix Two: Hits, Misses and Maybes   137

Further Reading   139

Glossary Of Spin Doctoring Terms   140

About The Author   144

1 Living In Spin

"Feared, loathed, venerated or emulated,
the spin doctors are amongst us,
moulding the images we see
and crafting the words we hear."

We live in the age of the spin doctor. The worlds of business, show biz, sport and most of all politics, are dominated by their activities. People, who may not even recognise the term, are influenced by the spin doctors. Commentators put the outcome of the British General Election of 1997 down to the activities of them. The Queen is reported to be looking for one. It is virtually impossible to open a newspaper without stories about them leaping out of the pages. Magazine profiles of them now jostle alongside profiles of stand-up comedians and celebrity chefs. Spin doctors are even portrayed in Hollywood blockbusters such as *'Primary Colours'* and *'Wag the Dog.'*

Feared, loathed, venerated or emulated, the spin doctors are amongst us, moulding the images we see and crafting the words we hear. Behind the scenes of politics and business, at the shoulders of the rich and powerful, discreetly out of camera shot (most of the time) and firmly off-the-record, they ply their trade.

Who are these powerful figures? 'Spin doctor' is a new term in British discourse. Most people are unclear exactly what a spin doctor is. The name has sinister connotations, as a manipulator, conspirator, propagandist, even a malign and evil force at the heart of the body politic.

> The *Chambers 21st Century Dictionary* defines spin doctor as *'someone, especially in politics, who tries to influence public opinion by putting a favourable bias on information presented to the public or to the media.'*

The modern spin doctor is more than just a propagandist or publicist. The role of the truly powerful spin doctor can be as an adviser, counsellor, and trusted friend to leaders.

Throughout history, powerful and influential people have had trusty lieutenants to represent them, speak for them, interpret their thoughts, and provide the masses with insight into their thinking and intent. The earliest examples were priests, explaining what was *really* meant by the commandments or religious texts. These figures acted as a buffer between leaders and led, providing advice and counsel to the great and the good, and rising and falling with them. Such a role confers huge influence and power on these figures.

The Age of the Spin Doctor

In the age of modern communications, the spin doctor has become an invaluable link between leaders in business, politics and public life and the consumers of media. It is through the media - newspapers, radio, television, Internet - that we view the world. In an age where no one attends public meetings to hear speeches, listens to debates in the House of Commons, or digests lengthy policy manifestos or a business prospectus, it is through the media that our reality is created. Those who can use the media to their advantage, can shape reality.

Spin doctors exist because there is no such thing as objective truth. Facts, figures, events, and words, all have different meanings to different people. So it is their interpretation that is the key issue. A famous television ad for the *Guardian* shows a skinhead running towards a businessman in the street. We assume the skinhead is a mugger, but actually he saves the businessman from falling masonry. The information presented to us plays on one set of prejudices and leads to make a set of assumptions, but the extra information changes our view by 180 degrees.

Perceptions can be changed by what you say and how you say it.

The people interviewed by TV investigator Roger Cook who try to stop the camera filming by sticking their hands over the lens look guilty before they've said a word (which is why Roger Cook does it). On the other hand you have the businessman wearing a sober suit and modest tie, interviewed in a book-lined office with a picture of his wife on the desk, who instantly commands authority and respect, even if he is the biggest crook on the planet.

The politician faced by journalists asking about a sex scandal who rushes into his car and hurriedly drives off already looks as though he has something to hide. The errant Government Minister photographed hiding his face in the backseat of a speeding car is convicted before he has time to present his case.

But a politician hit by a sex-scandal who appears with their entire family – wife, offspring, parents and all – at the garden gate of the family home, and offers the press pack a cup of tea with biscuits, is already speaking volumes about their wholesome home-life (somewhat disingenuously in the case of David Mellor).

Former MP Piers Merchant offered an interesting version of the family-at-peace photo opportunity, when he appeared at the family home with his wife, and his teenage mistress Anna Cox simultaneously. On a later occasion Miss Cox entertained the rat pack parked on Merchant's front drive by emerging from the house, going berserk at them, and being carted off in an ambulance twenty minutes later suffering from 'stress'. This is how *not* to deal with the media.

When Jack Straw's son was arrested for alleged possession of cannabis after being 'set up' by the *Mirror*, the way he and his spin doctors handled the potentially damaging crisis turned the situation to his advantage. By the *denouement* of the story, Jack Straw was a hero, speaking for the parents of teenagers everywhere, and a lone battler against gutter journalism. We should not be surprised that before the story broke, the aide Tony Blair dispatched to see Jack Straw in his south London home was not a legal expert or politician, but a spin doctor, Alastair Campbell. Another Labour spin doctor David Hill was dispatched to stay at Straw's side as the story broke. Unfortunately, Jack Straw's own personal spin doctor, Ed Owen, had chosen an inopportune time to take a holiday.

The way facts are presented adds to or detracts from their meaning. The spokesman on television may be making the most persuasive case imaginable, but our brains are picking up much more than the words -

his tie, his haircut, his accent, his stature, his surroundings, the books behind him, the company logo placed behind his left shoulder - all the overt and subliminal messages add to the impression we get from a thirty-second appearance on the television news. Why do some people on *Question Time* or *Newsnight* seem plausible and trustworthy, and others shifty and nervous?

The newspaper we read is filled with 'news' and 'comment' - but where does it come from, and who's pulling the strings? Why are some people suddenly famous and 'in the news', and why do the same names keep reappearing in the letters pages and Diary columns?

The answer is that nothing we see and hear in our newspapers, and magazines, or on radio and television got there by accident. Someone, somewhere took a decision to print or broadcast every second of exposure we receive. Everything which the media produces is the result of human effort - which means all that decision-making and effort can be manipulated. The skill of the spin doctor lies in knowing how, and crucially, when.

The term spin doctor was born, along with many of the techniques, in the United States of America. Spin doctor is an amalgam of 'spin' – the interpretation or slant placed on events (which is a sporting metaphor, taken from the spin put on a baseball by the pitcher, or the spin put on the cue-ball in pool), and 'doctor' deriving from the figurative uses of the word to mean 'patch-up', 'piece-together', and 'falsify'. The phrase first appeared in print in the New York Times during the 1984 US Presidential elections, and during the eighties the term became common amongst the political classes on both sides of the Atlantic, especially during the 1988 US Presidential elections.

John Anthony Maltese in *'Spin Control'*, a survey of US Presidential communications, says, *'Spinning a story involves twisting it to one's advantage, using surrogates, press releases, radio actualities, and other friendly sources to deliver the line from an angle that puts the story in the best possible light. Successful spinning involves getting the media to 'play along', by convincing them through briefings, backgrounders, or other methods of persuasion - that a particular spin to the story is the correct one.*

'Sometimes the spinner can accomplish the same result not by persuading reporters, but by simply making life easy for them...briefings and press conferences serve as a watering hole for packs of journalists in search of news...well choreographed photo-opportunities provide striking visual images that reinforce the messages that White House officials want to convey.'

Your Reputation Matters

But why should anyone bother? Hasn't all this obsession with style, spin and packaging gone too far? If the product you sell is good, or the message you say is true, surely people will accept you at face value? Wrong.

Whoever you are, your reputation matters. What people say about you, what they think, how you are valued and judged, all influence your success or failure in business, in careers, and in life. In the corporate world, reputation is increasingly seen as being as important an asset as capital or plant.

For many global firms reputation is *the* most important asset. They spend millions defending it. The recent McLibel trial, when the McDonalds corporation took a pair of environmental activists to court in a lengthy and costly case, shows the lengths business will go to. The McLibel Two were handing leaflets to people outside a London branch of McDonalds criticising the firm's environmental record. They were making as much impact on McDonalds' corporate reputation or burger sales as a snowflake landing in a volcano. Yet McDonalds took them to court, and drew worldwide attention to their cause. The McDonalds case against Helen Steele and David Morris cost £10 million and, at 315 days, was the longest ever civil trial in English history.

When the reputation of a company takes a knock, so does profits and share price.

 Gerald Ratner made one unguarded remark in front of an audience referring to his products as 'crap', and the business nearly collapsed.

✗   The greed of the directors of Camelot, the lottery organisers, in awarding themselves big bonuses led to a fall in lottery ticket sales and a drop in the BBC Lottery viewing figures.

✗   Any suggestion of contamination in foodstuffs - as happened to Perrier - can destroy years of advertising and public relations in a few days. Small traces of benzene were found in Perrier, and the product was recalled.

✗   The brand loyalty and status that Richard Branson has built over decades is threatened because of the failure of some Virgin trains to run on time.

Even places can suffer. Councillors in the Essex town of Basildon blame the lack of companies' investment in their town on the damage done by the previous MP David Amess, turning the name Basildon into a national laughing stock.

Careers, businesses, whole communities can be made and broken through the power of public opinion. Public opinion is moulded by the media. The media can be manipulated by spin. And that is where the spin doctor comes in.

In an age of virtually instant, 24-hour news coverage, there is often only a short time between an important event, speech, or announce-ment, and the subsequent news reports. The political spin doctor lives in that gap - between an event and its dissemination - and works to place the event in context, provide extra information, offer interpreta-tion and analysis, and to mould the way in which the event is reported. The spin doctor is there dealing with journalists, providing news and ideas, steering journalists in certain directions, and attempting to mould the media's output.

Let he that is without spin cast the first stone

These techniques are not confined to Presidents. The spread of spin doctoring is mirrored by the expansion in the communications business serving all kinds of organisations. In the late-eighties the public relations agency sector increased by over 100 per cent. The UK industry alone now turns over £1.2 billion each year and employs over 40,000 people. That's more than Britain's iron, steel, coal-mining and fishing industries combined. Over ten universities are now offering BA (Hons) or MSc in public relations and The Institute of Public Relations celebrated its fiftieth anniversary in 1998.

There are multi-million dollar international consultancies like Shandwick, Dewe Rogerson, Charles Barker, Burson-Marsteller and Hill and Knowlton making fortunes every year. And there are thousands of smaller companies offering specialist services in financial PR, consumer PR, or celebrity PR.

It is hard to think of a national organisation without an in-house team dedicated to spin. Everyone is at it:

> The League Against Cruel Sports and the Countryside Alliance,
> The Church of England and Palestine Liberation Organisation,
> Greenpeace and British Nuclear Fuels,
> The Chambers of Commerce and the Trades Union Congress.

They are all living in spin. Public relations exists whether we like it or not - any organisation, group or even individual interacts with others. Virtually every organisation you can think of employs someone to deal with the media, manage their reputation, and act as spokesperson. The quantity (and to be honest quality) of these 'PR Officers' 'Press Officers' and 'Media Relations Officers' varies. Not all are engaged in spin doctoring proper; some merely act as information officers. But the spin doctors are there nonetheless, crafting articles and news releases, manufacturing photo-opportunities, schmoozing journalists, and massaging your opinion.

The PR industry definition of public relations is *'the planned and sustained effort to establish and maintain goodwill and mutual understanding between an organisation and its publics'.*

That means that all organisations are engaged in attempts to make you aware of them, understand them, and give them love, respect, support, or money.

A Media Obsession

Spin doctoring has become a media obsession. In October 1997, the main political news story was the Government's decision on joining European Monetary Union. But the media were not exercised by the rights and wrongs of a single currency. The story focused on one man, a mobile phone, and a Friday evening in the Red Lion pub, Whitehall. The media became obsessed by the activities of the Chancellor's spin doctor Charlie Whelan, who became more newsworthy than the turbulence in the financial markets which he was alleged to have caused.

Journalists were dispatched to the Red Lion, location of Charlie Whelan's phonecall spinning to *Sun* and *Times* journalists. *Newsnight's* report on the affair was opened with the pop tune *'You spin me right round (like a record).'* Mr Whelan even earned the ultimate accolade: portrayal in a Steve Bell cartoon in the *Guardian* (now pinned up in the House of Commons Press Gallery.) The serious questions about EMU, which will affect fundamentally the way we live our lives were deemed less important by journalists than exposing Gordon Brown's awesome spin control.

In December 1997, spin doctors were in the news yet again, and given more prominence in some newspapers than their political masters. Alastair Campbell and Charlie Whelan were accused of not treating European journalists with enough respect during the lead-up to Britain's presidency of the European Commission, especially at the Luxembourg Summit. Carlos Segovia *of El Mundo* was reported as saying of Campbell: *'He laughed at us'*, while Pierre Bocev of *Le Figaro* said: *'if they wanted to be disliked, they could hardly do it in a better way.'* The reaction of those poor, placid foreign newspaper journalists to Blair's bully-boy spin doctors even merited a leader in the *Times*. Charlie Whelan dismissed the whole affair as *'Euro-bollocks'* (and he was probably right).

In January 1998, a biography of Chancellor Gordon Brown caused waves because of the implicit attacks on Prime Minister Blair - but it was not biographer Paul Routledge, nor Brown himself, who got the blame. It was Charlie Whelan, again.

Any history of the Labour Party is incomplete without reference to the first figure in Britain to be dubbed a spin doctor: Peter Mandelson. The former Lambeth councillor, TV producer and Director of Labour's

Communications became a famous player in eighties politics as Neil Kinnock's right-hand man. Many see Mandelson as the man who saved the Labour Party from collapse in the face of Margaret Thatcher's hegemonic grip on the British body politic. Peter Mandelson brought new communications techniques to a party whose relationship with the media and the public was at an all-time low.

Andy McSmith (who worked with Mandelson at the Labour Party press office) says of him in *Faces of Labour 'within an organisation long accustomed to the idea that second best will do, he displayed an exacting professional standard and demanded it from others'*. Within a year, the Tories viewed Mandelson with the same respect and fear that allied generals viewed Rommel.

After five years as Labour's Communications Chief, Mandelson was selected by the local Labour Party in Hartlepool to be their candidate, and he won the seat in 1992. His communications flair helped Tony Blair win the 1994 leadership contest (where his covert role was masked by the code-name 'Bobby'), and his campaigning brilliance guided Labour's 1997 landslide.

In the nineties, Peter Mandelson has become a leading political player in his own right, as Minister without Portfolio within the Cabinet Office, and one tipped for a place in the Cabinet before too long. And yet Peter Mandelson is in some ways a victim of his own success as a spin doctor. Despite a successful political career which has gone further and faster than a great many others, from local councillor to Government Minister, and the warmth and pride with which he is viewed by his traditional Labour constituents, he is still unable to shake off the tag of 'spin doctor'.

Behind every successful political leader there has to be a spin doctor. Previous Prime Ministers have employed the spin doctor's arts (before the phrase was even invented). Clem Atlee had Francis Williams, the former *Daily Herald* editor. Harold Macmillan had Harold Evans. Harold Wilson had Joe Haines and Gerald Kaufman. Margaret Thatcher had Bernard Ingham. Today, Tony Blair has Alastair Campbell.

- It may have been Jack Kennedy who said: *'ask not what your country can do for you, ask what you can do for your country.'* But it was Pierre Sallinger who put the words in his mouth.

- Margaret Thatcher may well have thought that Gorbachev was a *'man she could do business with'* but it was Bernard Ingham who invented the phrase and gave the quote to journalists.

● Tony Blair leads 'New Labour', but the expression, now an accepted part of political discourse and modern history, was invented by Peter Mandelson.

Spin doctors are no longer confined to politics. Behind every Richard Branson, David Beckham or Prince Charles is a spin doctor. The best ones are the ones you've never heard of. In the Labour Party everyone has heard of Alastair Campbell (spin doctor to Tony Blair) and Charlie Whelan (spin doctor to Gordon Brown). But one of the greatest contributors to Labour's communications strategy and daily spinning to the media over a twenty year period is a man few outside of the Westminster village have heard of - David Hill. That's because Hill, a consummate and respected professional, steers clear of all the temptations of magazine profiles and fly-on-the-wall documentaries. One of his few appearances in the media was being insulted by the Tory MP Alan Clark's *Diaries*, which is a compliment in itself.

But despite the degree to which the spin doctors are behind the scenes or in the limelight, they are there none-the-less, cajoling, bullying, and flattering the media on behalf of the great and the good.

Not everyone is a big fan of the spinners, of course.

Melanie Phillips, in the *Observer,* on 12 October 1997 called spin-doctoring *'a package of trickery, economies with the truth, manipulation of public credulity, bullying of journalists and favouritism.'*

A recent Gallop survey for the *Daily Telegraph* showed that in the minority of cases where people knew what a spin doctor was, terms such as *'liar', 'charlatan', 'manipulator',* and *'con artist'* were most commonly applied. Definitions included *'someone who phones out the gossip to the papers', 'a devious person', somebody who finds great difficulty in telling the truth',* and *'gives off a lot of hot air and is paid a lot of money'.* That negative image is not helped by people like Michael Shea whose political thriller *'Spin Doctor'* describes these modern Machiavellis as *'professional political strategists, able on behalf of their clients to manipulate the media - planting a story here, a rumour there, a tip-off somewhere else - so that any piece of news is tailored to show them in the best possible light.'* The first act of the spin doctor in Shea's novel is the framing with heroin smuggling of a woman threatening to embarrass a Tory minister. Not a particularly helpful portrayal.

Given the terrible reputation of the craft, perhaps it is a case of *'spin doctor – heal thyself.'*

The danger these sultans of spin face comes when the media become more interested in them than what they have to say. The 'shadowy background figures manipulating the media' have been subject to more media scrutiny than most MPs, popstars or premiership footballers. The *'men in the dark'*, to use Clare Short's memorable phrase, are all to often in the spotlight. Michael Cole, spinner-in-chief to Mohammed Al-Fayed until early 1998 is almost as famous as his former-boss. Indeed, they enjoyed equal billing on *Rory Bremner – Who Else?*. Charlie Whelan has been reputedly offered his own chat-show. Prince Charles's media strategist Mark Bolland is subject to full-page newspaper profiles. Bernard Ingham is a media celebrity and columnist, offering weekly advice in *PR Week*, and giving lucrative lectures to junior spin doctors.

Revealing the secrets of spin is an endeavour only slightly less risky than spilling the beans on the workings of Masonry. There are a lot of people making a lot of cash by selling their spin doctoring services to uninitiated, but wealthy, clients. Not all of them deserve it. As in any business, there are plenty of charlatans and snake-oil salesmen.

Dealing with the media is not rocket science. There are ground rules, and conventions. There are tricks of the trade and techniques. It can be learned.

Spin doctors are not just the glamour boys and girls of Westminster, the Square Mile, or Capitol Hill. Anyone can be a spin doctor. Local groups such as Parent Teacher Associations, Sunday league football teams, Community Health Councils, local shops and businesses, local trade union branches, Hospital leagues of friends, the local pub darts team, even a local church, temple, mosque or synagogue should appoint someone to deal with the media. For most organisations, media relations is not a matter of choice. If you're a company, hospital, charity, quango, university or public body the media will at some time or other come hunting for a story. For many other organisations, media relations is something they should be benefiting from, but usually they are not.

So - whether you want to protect the reputation of a FTSE-listed giant, get noticed by your promotion board, be talked about in your social circle, or simply want to see a review of your local AmDram production of the *Mikado* in the local rag, then get ready to spin.

2 Here Is The News...

"The most important attribute for the spin doctor is to understand journalists and the organisations they work for: what motivates them, what excites them, what annoys them and the pressures of the job that they suffer."

What Is News?

S pin doctors deal in news; they must understand what it is, and how it is made. The answer to the question 'what is news' is hotly contested and changes through time. One man's news is another's irrelevance, and what was considered news a hundred years ago is different from today. Some stories disappear without trace and some 'have legs' (i.e. they run and run.)

At its most basic, news is what journalists report. The problem is mirrored by the old late-night student conundrum *'if a tree falls down in a forest, with no-one there to hear it, does it make a noise?'* If something newsworthy happens and there is no journalist there to cover it, it is not 'news'. If TV news organisations do not have pictures to illustrate the story, then the item will be dropped. Arthur McEwan, editor of the *San Francisco Examiner* said *'news is whatever a good editor chooses to print.'*

There are several other differing definitions of news. Harold Evans former *Times* and *Sunday Times* editor said *"news is people. It is people talking and people doing."* And editor Arthur Christiansen advised his staff: *"always always always tell the story through people"*. An old boss of mine used to say: *'there's a story on every street corner.'*

Journalists have a shared sense of 'news-value' and there are common threads which can be discerned from most news stories. But journalists are also influenced by commercial imperatives, and the political slant of the publication. Papers have to be sold. Proprietors prejudices have be pandered to. Journalism can never be purely objective - there is always a context.

One view of 'what is news' is offered by the international newsagency Reuters: *'fires, explosions, floods...railway accidents, destructive storms, earthquakes, shipwrecks...accidents...street riots...strikes.... the suicide of persons of note, social or political, and murders of a sensational or atrocious character.'* That was issued by Reuters in 1883!

sense of news style has changed little

Denis MacShane in the seminal text for a generation of spin doctors *Using the Media* (1979) said news contained the following elements:
- ✔ conflict,
- ✔ hardship and danger to the community,
- ✔ unusualness (oddity, novelty),
- ✔ scandal,
- ✔ individualism.

This list covers most of what a journalist will turn into news.

Taking the newspapers for a single day, 28th November 1997, lets look for the elements of 'news' as MacShane defines them.

The Daily Mail's front page *is 'Woman's ordeal as rapist sued her for libel - astonishing move from his jail cell.'* This role reversal of victim and perpetrator is in the classic **unusualness** category. It's a case of 'dog bites man - that's not news. Man bites dog - now that *is* news.' There's a beast of Bodmin story on page three (**unusualness** again). Two political stories showing **conflict**: *'Labour MP's accuse Blair of bullying in Formula One row'* and *'Revolt over lone parent cash'*, and a dose of **scandal** *'The £3m backhander Saunders gave himself'*.

The *Daily Telegraph* runs *'120 Labour rebels challenge Blair'* (**conflict**), *'Guinness contempt for the truth'* (**scandal**), *'Rapist to sue'* (**unusualness**), and *'Blood fears'* a story about BSE in blood bank stock (**danger to the community**) all on the front page.

The *Express* leads with *'She's just a gold digger - Earl's friend lashes out at Victoria'*. The story - Earl Spencer's divorce - is an archetypal **conflict** story. They run the **scandal** of Earnest Saunders *'Greed, lies, and tricks of £3m crooked tycoon'*, and the **conflict** of *'120 Labour*

MPs rebel over lone parent cash'. *'Eat up your chips, girls'* is a story playing on the **unusualness** of a dietician saying girls should eat more junk food. *'How squadron leader bombed with sexy lover'* is a follow up of the **scandal** of a RAF officer on a murder charge, and there's more **scandal** with *'Bribes scandal hits Sandhurst'*.

The *Mirror* has plenty of **novel and odd** stories. *'Locked in passion'* is a story about a man handcuffed by his girlfriend for 'sex games' who lost the key and had to be freed by firemen. *'Pieces of Fright'* is about a parrot in a production of *'Treasure Island'* with stage fright. Then they run the **conflict** stories of Earl Spencer's divorce *'Vicious Greedy Liar!'* and *'Labour MPs blast Blair in tobacco ban blunder'* (nice use of alliteration, lads).

And lastly the *Sun* doesn't let us down in the **novelty and oddity** department with a story about a man who has undergone an operation to *'have his manhood expanded'*: *'I'm cock-a-hoop' Op turns 7.6in Erik into 100% sex machine'*. **Individualism** is displayed by a couple who chose two rabbits to be bridesmaids at their wedding: *'Let's get Hutched'*.

Another test of news value is the *'Hey Doris'* criteria, used by *Sun* journalist, Wendy Henry, during the eighties when the *Sun* was edited by Kelvin MacKenzie. Unless a story might provoke a *Sun* reader to exclaim to her friend: *'Hey Doris, take a look at this...'* the story didn't make it into the paper. The story about Erik and his new appendage passes the *'Hey Doris'* test with flying colours!

For most stories we might offer to journalists, especially on locals, we should be aiming to the pass the 'so what?' test. If the reaction to your story is 'so what?', then it's back to the drawing board. A surprising number of news releases sent to journalists, brimming with news of *'groundbreaking developments'* in tractor technology, or the latest thoughts of a middle manager in the frozen dessert business to the *'Puddings 2000'* conference in Harrogate, fail this simple test.

Spin doctors should share the journalists grasp of what makes a good story, not just to be able to give out stories, but also to spot danger signs and avoid damaging stories. You should understand what a hostile journalist can do with seemingly innocuous facts if they choose to do you over. A top-flight spin doctor can proudly point to the damaging stories he has *stopped* from appearing, as well the ones he has created.

All news has to be placed in context. The stories covered by the *Guardian* don't make it into the *Sun*. The stories in your local newspaper wouldn't appear in the *Times*. You have to be realistic about the story you are trying to tell, and decide whether it really is news-worthy enough to bother journalists with. You should also understand that once the story appears, it becomes public property, and hostile journalists might report it in ways that are not in your interest. Always think through how an enemy might use the information.

Who Are The Media?

The most important attribute for the spin doctor is to understand journalists and the organisations they work for: what motivates them, what excites them, what annoys them and the pressures of the job that they suffer. It is also vital to understand the news-gathering process and the structure of the media.

Journalists are not society's favourite creatures - they rank around lawyers and estate agents in the league of public esteem. Most, however, are hard-working, committed and intelligent. Journalists tend to have a sense of professionalism and pride in their job, which they see as an essential part of the democratic process. 'Freedom of the press', as the mark of a free society, is a concept they take seriously. Most have undergone specialist training, and have survived at the lower reaches of the profession on abysmal pay and conditions. The Guardian *Media Guide* describes the paths into the job as *'many and vague, usually mundane, and always badly paid.'*

The first step is to understand what kind of journalist you need to talk to. The job-title 'journalist' covers a multitude of sins, from the trainee (or 'cub') reporter on a local newspaper, to highly-paid and famous columnists on national newspapers such as Matthew Parris, Victor Lewis-Smith, Roy Hattersley, Julie Burchill, Paul Johnson, or Suzanne Moore. 'Journalist' also includes radio reporters, television researchers, freelancers and those working on trade and technical titles. Each of these 'types' of journalist have widely different agendas, requirements, pressures and specialisms.

There are two main forms of media: Print and Broadcast. Print includes all newspapers and magazines and news agencies, and broadcast includes all television, radio, Teletext and Internet.

Many of the methods of news-gathering and production are similar across both media, and some journalists work in print and broadcast at the same time, or skip between the two camps. For example Simon Buckby was a producer for LWT and the BBC, and is now social affairs correspondent on the *Financial Times*. John Kampner has gone in the opposite direction, leaving the FT to join the BBC. There are, however, distinct differences between the two, and a spin doctor needs to understand them.

A love-hate relationship

Journalists and spin doctors have a healthy disdain for one another; each group believes themselves to be superior; yet neither could operate without the other. They are two sides of the news-creation coin.

Most spin doctors have worked as journalists:

- Joe Haines and Gerald Kaufman (Harold Wilson's spin doctors) worked on the *Mirror*.

- Bernard Ingham worked on the *Yorkshire Post*. In 1986 Ingham expressed his empathy with journalists (rather like a cheetah expressing empathy with the gazelle)*:* *'I feel for the reporter... I have shared with him his perishing funerals, his sodden agricultural shows, his grisly murders, his eerie ghost hunts, his endless doorsteps.'*

- Alastair Campbell was political editor on the *Mirror* and deputy editor on *Today*.

- Peter Mandelson was a TV producer at London Weekend Television working on *Weekend World* with Brian Walden, and for a brief time, a columnist on the *People* (In 1997 he remarked in a speech to House of Commons Lobby journalists that his column was said to be written by more people than read it.)

The experience of working in the news-gathering process is useful in the control and dissemination of information via the media. Alastair Campbell's ability to dream up telling phrases that find echo in the headlines of the tabloids is legendary. (It was Campbell who put the words *'People's Princess'* in the mouth of Tony Blair on the morning after Diana's death – a phrase which is now common currency).

The traffic is less heavy the other way: from spin doctor to journalist. But some have made the journey. Simon Buckby used to spin for John Prescott and now works at the *Financial Times*, Derek Draper was right-hand man to Peter Mandelson and now is a successful *Express* columnist and author, and even Thatcher's spin doctor Bernard Ingham now has gone back to journalism as a columnist.

To be a successful spin doctor you must know what gets journalists' juices flowing, and what makes them want to slam the phone down. You have to be able, in the words of Harper Lee, '*to stand in their shoes and walk around.*'

Print

National newspapers

When we talk of the 'press', national newspapers are what most people think of. The national newspapers carry huge authority and influence, and carry the best, and worst, of British journalism. Two thirds of the British public read a national newspaper every day. This figure has fallen from twenty years ago when almost 80 per cent of the adult population read a daily paper, and the newspaper market has become increasingly bitterly contested - with the circulation war having a profound effect on newspaper design, content and standards of journalism.

There are ten national daily newspapers. They can be divided into populars ('pops') or tabloids ('tabs'): (*Sun, Mirror, Daily Star*), mid-markets (*The Express, Daily Mail*) and the broadsheets (*Guardian, Times, Financial Times, Daily Telegraph, Independent*).

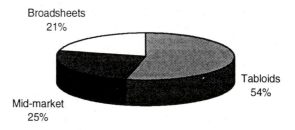

Approximate market share of daily newspaper types

Added to these are the national Sunday newspapers: *News of the World, Sunday Mirror, Mail on Sunday, People, Sunday Times, Express on Sunday, Sunday Telegraph, Observer, Sunday Business* and the *Independent on Sunday*. Two other titles are national and appear in newspaper format - the *Morning Star* (the Communist daily) and the *Daily Sport* (a comic). Also the London *Evening Standard* which has a huge readership and enormous influence, can be bought in most UK cities, but is technically a regional paper.

There has been a trend towards concentration of ownership. The national newspaper business is controlled by seven owners:

News International (Rupert Murdoch's lot)
• *Sun* • *Times* • *News of the World*

Mirror Group
• *Mirror* • *Sunday Mirror* (and, until March 1998, a stake in)
• *Independent* • *Independent on Sunday,*

United News and Media
• *Express* • *Express on Sunday* • *Star*

Daily Mail and General Trust
• *Daily Mail* • *Mail on Sunday* • *Evening Standard*)

The Telegraph (controlled by Conrad Black)
• *Daily Telegraph* • *Sunday Telegraph*

Guardian Media Group
• *Guardian,* • *Observer*

Pearson
• *Financial Times*

Readerships vary greatly between these newspapers. The *Sun* sells around 4 million copies, and is read by over ten million. The *Financial Times* sells around 300,000 copies.

Yet for the spin doctor, it is not just a numbers game.

More important than the raw circulation figures is an understanding of which social class and profession tends to read it. Also, newspapers have their own political slant: the *Mirror* is Labour, whilst the *Daily Telegraph* is Tory.

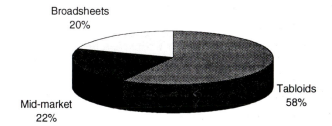

Approximate market share of Sunday newspaper types

A financial spin doctor will target the *FT* because of the people who read it (business leaders, investors etc), rather than the volume. But political spin doctors recognise the value of mass circulation tabloids like the *Sun* for spreading a political message to millions. The Buckingham Palace press office, for instance, has chosen the *Sun* to leak exclusive details of the Royal Family's Way Ahead Group deliberations on modernising the monarchy, because of its massive readership.

When politicians want to communicate messages to their own parties, they might choose newspapers which are read by party members. An article placed in the *Guardian* will reach most of the Labour Party membership, despite that newspaper's hostility to the Labour Party. Similarly, whenever the Tories have something to say to Tories, they tend to choose the *Daily Telegraph* (or the *Torygraph*, as *Private Eye* calls it), or perhaps the *Daily Mail*.

Broadsheets tend to be more believed, and carry more weight than tabloids. But if you want to know what people will be talking about on the bus to work or in the staff canteen, read the tabloids.

Local papers

Local newspapers are more important than you might think. There are over 100 daily local and regional newspapers and 1,300 weeklies in the UK. Even the freesheet shoved through your letter box gets audiences in tens of thousands. Freesheets can also reach audiences in the hundreds of thousands. (*Manchester Metro News*'s circulation is over 300,00; *Nottingham Post and Recorder*: 180,000; *Southampton Advertiser*: 130,000).

If you're one of those people who complains that 'they're all adverts' then you should be asking why so many advertisers pay hard cash to place ads. It's not for love. It's because local papers are read by enough people to make advertising worthwhile. Local weekly and daily newspapers attract over £2 billion of advertising revenue per year (only television attracts more) and 88 per cent of adults read their local paper.

Forty per cent of adults claim to prefer their local paper to the nationals.

These papers can have huge readerships. The London *Evening Standard* is bought by over 450,000 people every day in the Greater London area (more than people reading the *Guardian, Independent* and *Financial Times* in the whole UK.)

The *Birmingham Evening Mail* is bought by nearly 200,000 people, *the Manchester Evening News* has a circulation of over 180,000. Actual readership figures are even higher for all papers, as copies are left on the bus, in the pub, or around the kitchen table for others to read.

So let us hear no more about them being unimportant or not mattering. If a mention in the *Liverpool Echo* can reach 165,000 people in a single day, the locals and regionals matter to the spin doctor. This is especially true of local politicians or MPs, who know their voters will read the local papers, and spend hours courting the *Hartlepool Mail* or the *Billericay Recorder*.

Often the smaller titles such as the *Yellow Advertiser* in South Essex are staffed by just one or two news journalists, making them great targets. The journalists tend to be young, first- or second-jobbers, and keen to make their mark. Most stay on the paper for only a year or two, and most dream of a job on a national newspaper. They appreciate being offered good local stories and quotes, and will keep coming back for more.

If your targeting is right, your story has a strong local angle, and your news release is well-written, you have a good chance of success. Sometimes your words will appear verbatim. I once sent a news release to a freesheet who not only printed the text word-for-word, but also the news release instructions to the subs including '*ends*' and '*for more information contact Paul Richards...*'

The local angle is the key, though. If the story is about an event in the wrong part of town or wrong village (off "the patch"), the journalist won't touch it. Garath Weekes the editor of the *Salisbury Journal* put it well: *'world shattering events could be happening in Devizes...but not a line would appear in the* Salisbury Journal *because our world ends at the village of Upavon'*.

Local papers want a steady diet of local stories about local people, events, or places. Local campaigns and pressure groups can do well; or local interest groups like the local history society, local hospital league of friends, and local teams and clubs.

My first job on the *Buckinghamshire Advertiser* was to go through the 'Deaths' announcements in the national newspapers, spot any local people who had died, and phone their grieving families to see if there was a story. I was sixteen at the time, and understandably balked at this ghoulish task, but the editor made me do it anyway. *'If you can't do this,'* he said, *'forget being a journalist'*.

The way local journalists carry out this unpleasant task, incidentally, is to phone the next-of-kin and claim that you are writing a special tribute to the deceased ('a respected and loved local figure'). What they are really after is to discover if the deceased was found wearing women's underwear with a bag on their head and an orange stuffed in their mouth.

Often local papers have a 'comment' or 'soap box' page for readers to share their thoughts. Recent subjects covered by the 'Soapbox' section in the *Hammersmith Gazette*, for example, have included everything from European Monetary Union, to fluoride in the water. These columns are prime targets for spin.

Magazines

There has been an explosion of titles in the magazine sector in the last twenty years. In the last decade the number of magazines produced has increased by a third, and circulation has increased by over ten per cent. Magazines are now available for every leisure and lifestyle interest, from women's magazines like *Cosmopolitan, Elle, Prima, She, Woman's Own*, to consumer titles like *Good Housekeeping, BBC Good*

Food magazine, Radio Times, .Net and *Family Circle*, and 'new lad' magazines like *Loaded* and *FHM*. There are also current affairs and political magazines which reach important audiences, like *New Statesman, Spectator*, and the *Economist*. The top-selling magazines have readerships in the millions (*Sky TV Guide*: over three million; *Readers Digest*: 1.5 million; *Radio Times*: nearly 1.5 million).

The news content of these magazines is minimal, and the lead-times for publication may be months. The approach you make is very different from contacting a news room. Magazines use freelancers for most of their material, and so the relationship you need to develop with the journalist is harder to pin down. If you want to place stories and features in magazines, you need to plan months in advance, and place material which suits the style and content of the target title.

An article on homelessness might make it into *New Statesman*, but won't even get read at *Maxim*. A story about a group of women mountaineers climbing Mount Everest would be of interest to *Cosmopolitan*, but not to *Loaded* (unless they were climbing it naked). Magazines want human interest, not hard news. Politicians can appear in these magazines, but usually in a non-political context. The spin doctor can place features about politicians' love of classic cars, or at home in their beautifully restored seventeenth century cottage, but not about their latest speech to the CBI.

The benefit of having your message appear in these lifestyle and consumer magazines is that people tend to be less cynical and sceptical about what they read in magazines. A serious message which appears in a consumer mag has greater impact. Political parties have begun to target these titles, especially women's magazines, because it can reach audiences in ways which traditional news media have exhausted.

During the 1992 General Election the Labour Party produced a mock women's magazine filled with frothy stories and big pictures which activists were supposed to go about the country leaving in hairdressers and dentists. The cover star, in jeans and open-neck shirt, was a rising star called Tony Blair. In the 1997 General Election, great use was made by Labour of 'advertorials' – the paid-for features which masquerade as real articles in magazines.

Trades and technicals

These tend to appear as the 'joke' title in the missing words round *of 'Have I Got News for You'*, but for many thousands of journalists publications like *British Baker* and *Dairy Farmer* are their bread and butter.

Amateur Gardening, Angling Times, Bee World, Bird Watching, The Budgerigar, Flying Saucer Review, Freemasonry Today, The Grocer, Helicopter International, Local Historian, Manchester United Magazine, Materials Reclamation Weekly, Municipal Journal, Office Equipment News, Packaging Week, Pig Farming, Rugby World, Shoe and Leather News, Sporting Gun, Structural Engineer, Timber Trades Journal, Water Bulletin, Which Motorcaravan, Your Cat, and finally *Zionist Review* are magazines which delight, amuse and make the day of millions of people. These titles are also eagerly awaited by thousands of people in the relevant business or trade, as a source of unique information and news.

When I worked at the Urban Regeneration Agency, the *Guardian* and *Times* were often left unread in the press office, and they didn't even bother ordering the *Sun* and the *Mirror,* but the usually responsible quango-crats would fight like dogs over the weekly magazine *Urban Environment Today.* The same is true of every trade magazine - they are all loved by someone, otherwise they wouldn't be published. The Labour Party's Millbank HQ in the 1997 general election dedicated press officers to targeting these trades and technicals, because of their importance.

This means that a story which falls into the realm of these titles stands a good chance of being taken seriously, because the journalist has a whole magazine to fill, and no individual subject area is that interesting. Usually, however, the technical understanding is high, and your story must have some depth to it. The readers will have a high level of specialist knowledge about the subject. A large number of people think their organisation's new website will be instantly newsworthy to *Computer Weekly*, but usually it is not.

Broadcast

Television

In terms of mass communication, television is the most powerful medium - that's why advertisers spend millions to promote their products on television. After all, a visual image is far more powerful than the printed word. Ninety-seven per cent of UK households have a TV set, 64 per cent have two and 28 per cent have three or more. **On average, around forty per cent of leisure time is spent watching TV.** So, spin doctors take TV very seriously indeed because of this potency.

In Britain the TV sector breaks down like this:

- Public sector (the BBC) which is funded via the TV licence fee and broadcast nationally;

- Private sector (ITV) funded by advertising revenue broadcast regionally on 16 local stations and nationally on Channel Four and Channel Five; and

- Satellite and cable which is funded by adverts and subscriptions.

BBC 1 enjoys over thirty per cent of audience share, BBC 2 and Channel 4 both have about 10 per cent, and the ITV regional stations like Carlton and Granada have between one and five per cent each. Cable stations like the Disney Channel, Cartoon Network, UK Gold, Bravo and QVC have below one per cent each.

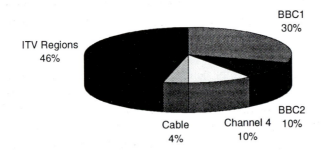

Approximate audience share of terrestrial TV channels

In our times, television has undergone a revolution. Gone are the days when TV meant a choice of three channels; today people can access hundreds. Since the eighties we have seen the launch of Channel Four, Channel Five, breakfast TV, the introduction of cable and satellite, and the BBC's 24-hour news programme.

The proliferation of channels has not meant a proliferation of news reporting on television, but there are opportunities for spin doctors. Stations like Sky News, BBC News 24, and cable channels like L!ve TV have a great deal of airtime to fill. They have an insatiable appetite for talking heads, and can be targeted for interviews and comment.

Television news programmes remain the best target for spin doctors and the daily bulletins are monitored closely by the political parties, and producers phoned if they sense any bias or omissions.

The most important are the
- 5.40 ITN news, and
- 6.00pm BBC news bulletins,

and then the
- 7.00pm Channel 4 News,
- 9.00pm BBC, and
- 10.00pm ITN bulletins.

These news programmes are known in the business by the times they start. You should refer to 'the Nine' or the 'the Six', if you want to sound like you know what you're talking about. You can spot the spin by following the progress of a particular story on these bulletins during a day. The coverage may change from lunch-time to tea-time, and to evening as the story develops, new interviews are edited in, new angles appear, and the spin doctors have gone to work.

The rolling 24-hour news on Sky News has an importance for spin doctors beyond its audience share. It is also followed by all the other news organisations as stories develop. Newsrooms will have Sky News on all day. At Millbank Tower, Labour's election nerve centre, Sky News was on constantly. During the 1997 general election, Labour used Sky to break stories and give interviews because the spin doctors knew the rest of the media would be watching. They used Sky almost like a news wire service, putting information into every newsroom in the country.

The local television stations have local news operations which can be targeted with good local stories with plenty of visual interest. The same rule applies as for local papers – it must be local to even be considered.

Programmes such as *Newsnight* and *World in Action* maintain high standards of journalism on terrestrial TV, and remain the most difficult programmes to influence, as competition is fierce. Other programmes like *Kilroy* and *The Time, The Place* have studio audiences which are easy to get people into, especially if you have something interesting or controversial to say. In the past, people have been exposed masquerading as 'serial guests' on these programmes, wearing disguises and pretending to be reformed criminals, drug addicts, or single parents.

The next big change to hit television is the move to digital broadcasting, which will replace current analogue technology within ten years. There are fears that digital broadcasting will increase the costs of viewing, and exclude some people from the plethora of channels and services which the new technology will allow. What it will mean is that television will become more interactive, be used for home shopping and banking, and cease to be a medium which chooses what you watch and when. Instead, television programmes and films will become available on demand (thus wiping out the video industry?)

Radio

Like television, the structure of the radio industry is split between the BBC and the commercial sector, and organised on a national and local level. There are five national BBC stations, and a handful of national commercial stations including Classic FM, Talk Radio and Virgin 1215.

The BBC has prestige programmes like *Today* and *The World at One*, which set the news agenda and reach important opinion-forming audiences.

The country is covered in local radio stations. Each major town has a BBC station and a commercial station, for example York has *BBC Radio York*, and *Minster FM*; Manchester has *GMR* (the BBC) and *Key 103*.

Although the figure has dipped slightly in the latter half of the nineties, 85 per cent of over-fifteens listen to the radio at least once a week. All radio stations carry an element of news. The BBC has its major international news operation, using reporters in common with television as part of its 'bi-media' approach.

The 38 BBC local radio stations use news fed from the national operation, and from their own newsdesks. They are supplied material from the GNS (the General News Service) which makes live interviews available to a range of local stations one after the other from a single studio. Commercial radio uses their own reporters and Independent Radio News (IRN), based at the ITN headquarters. Stations like Talk Radio, Radio Five Live, and London's News Direct rely on a constant supply of interviewees. Local radio needs local stories on the same criteria as local papers - with the obvious exception that radio needs people to talk about the story.

The smaller stations have very few staff, especially at the weekends, and so it is important to make the right approach. You can make a world of difference between phoning at five minutes to the hour, when the news presenter is desperately finishing off scripts for the hourly news bulletin, and five minutes after the hour when the bulletin is over and the presenter has time to talk to you. Radio newsrooms have separate phone numbers from the main switchboard numbers, so if you need to phone them over a weekend or after hours, you need the right number.

News Agencies

A news agency is a news-gathering organisation which sells its news and information to print and broadcast media. National and international agencies such as the Press Association, Associated Press, Bloomberg Business News or Reuters serve newsrooms and other organisations via an on-line link-up, still known as a 'wire'. *'What's running on the wires?'* means what stories are appearing from the news agencies. Smaller agencies might specialise in subject areas (e.g. Computerwire, RaceNews), or be based on a specific geographical area (e.g. Bournemouth News and Print Services, Anglia Press Agency).

The Press Association (PA) is the main news agency in the UK, jointly owned by the national newspapers. It has a vital role in the creation of news, and is therefore of great importance in the world of spin doctoring. The Press Association is not a media outlet in its own right - it supplies news stories and information via on-line computers. They employ staff reporters, specialist correspondents, photographers, feature writers and editors the same as a national newspaper. It also has a new radio service.

News stories appear on the screen under 'snaps' or 'slugs' or short headings, with the time they were written or the embargo on their use, and are supplied direct to newsrooms, businesses, and Parliament. Even some posh London clubs, like the Reform, have PA (still supplied via a telex onto sheets of paper which are pinned up on a board). Subscribers to PA can then use the material in their own publications - either wholesale, or as the basis for their own reporting of the story. PA also supplies photos on-line, diary dates, and quotes.

I was the lowly Labour Party press office apparachik assigned to Tony Blair for a day in summer 1993 when the great man was Shadow Home Secretary. We caught wind of a breaking news story about a prisoner dying in the back of a van whilst in the custody of the private firm, Group 4. Tony Blair's second thought, after sympathy for the man's family, was to get a quote (*'the Group 4 farce has turned to tragedy'*) on the PA wire as soon as possible, because of the importance of PA in shaping a breaking news story. If you have something worth saying, you can usually by-pass the PA reporters and get straight through to 'copy-takers' who will input your quote or statement immediately (just ask for 'copy'). PA also receives a blizzard of news releases on a minute-by-minute basis, and has a healthy disregard for most of them.

If a story, quote or event appears on PA, it appears in the newsrooms of virtually every important media outlet in the country. It can mean that a single phone-call to PA can lead to coverage in dozens of newspapers, national and regional, and be picked up for further coverage by the broadcasters.   PA is instrumental in breaking news stories. The death of Princess Diana, and John Major calling the election are examples of stories where PA got it first.

Different Types Of Journalist

As discussed before, 'journalist' covers a variety of different functions within the media.

The structure of a newsroom on a newspaper is designed along Fordist production lines: each part of the process is carried out by a different person, with different specialists contributing different parts to the whole. With broadcast, the process is less defined. Within the BBC, journalists can work for both radio and television ('bi-media') on a specialist area such as politics, economics or religious affairs. A story on a major court case verdict will be covered by legal affairs editor Joshua Rosenberg on the BBC radio *Today* programme at 8am, and on the BBC TV lunchtime news at 1pm by the same person.

Here are the main types of journalist in print, radio, and TV.

Reporter

At the front line is the reporter - responsible for writing news stories, or delivering reports direct on radio or TV. On a local paper there might be only a handful; on a national newspaper, hundreds. This is the type of journalist most people feel they understand the best: the fearless crusader for truth; the tireless scribe; the investigator of injustice. When people have any kind of direct contact with journalists, it is the reporter they usually face. Reporters have been immortalised in fiction, from Lois Lane and Clarke Kent on the *Daily Planet*, to Damien Day, the unscrupulous TV news reporter in *Drop the Dead Donkey*. Writers such as Charles Dickens and Rudyard Kipling started as reporters. Even Winston Churchill had a spell as a reporter.

Specialist Correspondent

A journalist covering a particular area such as health, sport, personal finance, cooking or defence. They will have job titles like 'Health Corespondent' or 'Sports Editor'.

News Editor

This is a more senior position, responsible for allocating stories to reporters, deciding priorities and angles and usually reporting to the editor. Often a journalist with a few more years' experience, but who has been promoted through the ranks of news reporters, and will still write news stories.

Sub-Editor

This is a specialist function, and my favourite type of journalist. The sub-editors ('subs') receive the reporter's articles ('copy') via the newspaper's computer system, and 'weave their magic' (if you believe the subs) or 'hack it to pieces' (if you believe the reporters). The subs job is to check spelling, grammar, house-style, and length of the piece, all of which they might change. They also write captions for photographs, 'panels' (the sections of text pulled out of an article and placed between two lines, used to break up long articles) 'standfirsts' (the text between the headline and the main text, often used on features and longer news pieces.) The subs also layout the page.

Subbing might be extremely heavy, in the case of a tabloid newspaper where space is at a premium, or lighter on a weekly title. They might speak to the reporter for clarification, or refer the article to the lawyers for legal checking. As reporters develop their skills on a particular newspaper, the need for subbing becomes less, as they automatically write to suit the newspaper's own house style.

Subs are also the heroes of the headline. On the tabloids, where daring, attention-grabbing headlines are the most important part of the paper, the subs' craft can be best seen. *'Gotcha',* and *'Freddy Starr Ate my Hamster'* and the daily puns and screaming headlines in the *Sun* and *Mirror* are the product of a sub's fevered brain.

Three cheers for the subs who bring us headlines like *'Top Tory flops for the chop'* (a story about the Shadow Cabinet Reshuffle, *News of the World* 30th November*), 'My briefs encounter with bare bot Anne'* (about a sexual harassment case involving a knicker-less council employee, Sun 28th November), *Driver is a trifle care-less* (an idiot driver was seen negotiating a roundabout while eating a sherry trifle with a spoon *Sun* 30th December) and *Just the Ticket* (bus workers were last night celebrating a whopping festive pay rise *Daily Record* 30th December).

The stone sub is the senior sub who makes the final corrections and checks.

There is a move in some quarters to streamline the process of reporting and subbing, by combining the roles. The *European* newspaper is moving in this direction. The *Bradford Telegraph and Argus* tried an 'orbital system' with reporters, subs and designers working together as a team on subject areas such as health or consumer. The result, according to one insider, was a 'nightmare' and they have reverted to more traditional divisions of labour.

Editor

On a newspaper the Editor is the boss with whom the buck stops. They will be a journalist of many years standing, and seek to influence the overall style, content and tone of the paper. Usually the Editor will report directly to the owner of the paper – the relationship between an editor and proprietor is similar to a football manager and the owner of the club. On the nationals, the Editor can become a famous figure in their own right, such as Kelvin MacKenzie, Andrew Marr, Andrew Neil, or Andreas Whitam-Smith. The hiring and firing of Editors can become news in itself, for example when Andrew Marr was ousted from his position at the Independent in January 1998, and reinstated as editor-in-chief in March 1998.

In TV and Radio, the Editor is in overall charge of a particular programme or series. They are responsible for the overall tone and content, and take the rap if something goes wrong or provokes complaints.

Section Editor

On a newspaper, different parts of the paper will have separate editors, for example the Business Pages editor, the Women's Pages editor, or the colour supplement editor.

Producer

In radio and TV, the producer is responsible for the technical production of a programme or section of a programme (a 'package'). There is a move in TV towards multi-skilled producer/reporters who produce the segment of a programme, and also provide the on-screen comment and 'sign-off' at the end.

Assistant Producer (AP)

This is a more junior version of producer, working for a producer, and often learning on the job. The role should not be confused with that of **Production Assistant (PA)** who is the person (usually young and female) responsible for the administrative side of programme-making such as booking cars for guests, sorting out locations, expenses and ordering the sandwiches.

Researcher

These are the people in TV, usually young and thrusting, who provide the ideas, planning and research for programmes. They are the people who will read news releases, monitor the newspapers and rival stations, spot trends and come up with imaginative ideas. They tend to be starting out in the business, and want to be promoted to APs or reporters.

Freelances

Journalists who sell their services to different news organisations, but are not directly employed. The National Union of Journalists produces a handy annual directory of freelance journalists, with contact details and favoured subjects. Freelances earn their living by constantly producing enough material to sell to editors. It is a precarious way to make a living. If they can develop regular work, in a specialist field such as social services, or as a political pundit like Sion Simon (regular writer for the *Telegraph* and *Spectator*) the rewards can be great.

Columnists

Journalists who write a personal column or page in a newspaper or magazine, setting out their view of current events, what they've been up to that week, which parties they went to, and so on. Columnists include Roy Hattersley (*Guardian*), Polly Toynbee (*Guardian*), Norman Tebbit (*Sun*), Derek Draper (*Express*) Peter McKay (*Daily Mail*) Anne Robinson (*Mirror*) and the late Jeffrey Bernard (*Spectator*). In magazines, columnists might be specialists in their fields, for example Bernard Ingham's column in *PR Week*. The genre is sent up effectively in the *Guardian* by the fictitious Bel Littlejohn, who apparently receives fan mail and real complaints.

3 Dealing With The Media

"It is possible to be friendly with journalists,
but never believe they can be your friends."

Getting It Right:
What do journalists want?

When dealing direct with journalists, professionalism and skill is required, as most of them are nobody's fool. You can have the greatest news release writing skills, can dream up brilliant stunts, photo-opps, and stories, but all of it will count for nothing if you don't have credibility with journalists. Part of the skill of a journalist is being able to sniff out a time-waster on the end of a phone and get rid of them, and by the same token, spot a fellow professional who may be of some use in filling that blank space on page four. These are basic ground-rules in dealing with the media:

Spoon feeding

The basic job of the spin doctor is to help journalists create news. Journalists do not have the time for interpreting complex data or reading lengthy reports, and this is a great opportunity to 'help' the journalist in their job by providing handy summaries and crib-sheets (resplendent with 'interpretation and background', naturally).

You must be clear about what you mean, understand what makes a story, have understandable background information, facts, photos and graphics available, and be capable of getting this into the hands of a journalist as soon as possible: by fax or by motorcycle courier. A charitable view of journalists may be that they spend their time chasing leads, checking sources, and ferreting out the truth, but with a deadline looming and pressure to find a story, they are not averse to a little spoon feeding from spin doctors.

Speed kills

Understand that journalists are working to deadlines, with editors breathing down their necks. If a journalist phones you for some information or a quote, they need answers within minutes, not days. Beating your spin doctoring opponent means being faster than them. The slogan 'speed kills' appeared on the wall of the Clinton War Room during the US Presidential elections in 1992. Under the direction of James Carville and George Stephanopolous (the spin doctors' spin doctors), the Clinton camp had their reaction to events so finely tuned that they could have the Clinton response and rebuttal to a George Bush speech with journalists before Bush even sat down. That meant that time and time again, the news story was not what Bush had said, but what Clinton was saying about what Bush has said.

As a news story develops, especially in the 24-hour world of radio and TV, the angle of the story can be altered by new information on a minute by minute basis. The way journalists use interviews during the cycle changes hour by hour. In a disaster situation the first bulletins feature eye witnesses. Later bulletins feature interviews with the emergency services. Later on, the airline whose plane has crashed, or the country where the earthquake happened will deploy spokesmen. Last to appear, on *Newsnight* and the *World Tonight*, will be 'experts' on flight safety, terrorism, earthquakes, hostage psychology or food poisoning, depending on the disaster.

Spin doctors need to understand deadlines. For a huge news story, front pages can be altered, and news bulletins changed at the last minute. Newspapers can change layout from edition to edition on the same day - or even produce special editions to cover a major story such as the death of a Royal. News bulletins can be interrupted during broadcast with a major news story. But this is the exception, not the rule. To influence the news agenda, you have to be ahead of the game, and that means operating well in advance of deadlines. For a daily newspaper, you should aim for late afternoon the previous day, at the very latest. For a Sunday, it should be Friday afternoon. Weekly magazines can take news 3-4 days in advance of publication, but will have their features worked out weeks in advance. Glossy monthlies like *Cosmopolitan* are designed months in advance.

The deadline is the last possible moment, and there are other important staging posts before that. On a daily newspaper, reporters have to inform their news editors what stories they will be filing, so that space can be allocated, by mid-afternoon. Earlier still, at around 11am, the senior reporters will gather for a news conference to map out the days events. Your event, speech, or stunt must be lodged into the newspaper's system by these times to stand a chance of coverage.

Honesty is the only policy

If journalists detect dishonesty or subterfuge, their trust will soon evaporate, and the game is up. There is no point whatever in lying to journalists. That is not to say that you have to tell the entire truth all the time, or let all the facts get in the way of a good story. Knowing which bits of the truth to reveal, when, and to whom, is the art of the spin doctor. The spin doctor should know all the facts, but never completely reveal his hand.

The saga of Home Secretary Jack Straw's son being arrested in a good example of this. The sequence of events is roughly as follows: 17-year old William Straw is targeted by two *Mirror* journalists who ask him to purchase some cannabis. Before the story is revealed by the *Mirror*, Straw senior marches young William into the police station where he is arrested. The case then becomes *sub-judice*, meaning that identity of the son cannot be revealed by the *Mirror*. Labour's spin doctors release the story of an unnamed Cabinet Minister behaving in a thoroughly responsible fashion in dealing with every middle-class parents' nightmare, but Straw's identity remains secret from the public. By the time the name of the Minister is finally revealed, every journalist, politician and *cognoscenti* knows it is Straw because they have worked it out, so the impact is lessened. The sting is taken out of the story. Through his honesty and guts, Straw becomes a hero. The *Mirror* is painted as the villain. One of the journalists, Dawn Alford, is even arrested. Score at the final whistle? Hacks nil, Spin Doctors 5.

If Jack Straw had attempted to lie, to stonewall, to whitewash or cover-up, we would have had a new Home Secretary within days.

No 'No Comment'

There no such thing as 'no comment', and hoping a story will go away. Saying 'no comment' is the act of someone who watches too much television. It is as removed from the real world of news as journalists with a label marked 'press' sticking out of the band in their hats, and people in newsrooms shouting *'hold the front page'*.

To a journalist, 'No comment' means *'the only comment I have to make is that I am guilty of something, have something to hide, or am engaged in a major cover-up, so you had better chase this story like your life depends on it.'* In other words, *'No comment'* is a red rag to a bull.

There can also be dangers in issuing straightforward denials, because the denial can provide a peg for the story (*'So-and-so angrily denied reports last night that he was a heroin-addict'*).

The spin doctor must be able to comment and deal with adverse publicity as well as the good stuff. The best examples of 'crisis management' are when the polluting oil company or retailer caught selling poisonous cat food has been as open and honest as possible. Open public relations and genuine contrition can turn a situation round.

Access to the Organ Grinder

Usually the spin doctor is the conduit for information between the journalist and a senior figure, or the *'sewer, not the sewage'*, as John Biffen once said of Bernard Ingham. Often the spin doctor acts as a lightening conductor for their boss, taking the flak and diverting criticism.

In the USA, political spin doctors like James Carville and George Stephanopoulous can even take part in public debates and media appearances themselves, as commentators in their own right. We have yet to see that development over here, thank heavens. (Although there are plenty of former spin doctors like Bernard Ingham, Michael Shea, even Derek Draper, who have cashed in their chips and become authors, columnists and pundits). There are moves in that direction, now that the Prime Minister's spokesman Alastair Campbell can be quoted 'on-the-record' rather than the old-fashioned formula of 'Downing Street sources' or 'sources close to the Prime Minister'.

But the practising spin doctor must not be a barrier, and from time to time must facilitate access to his or her boss for hacks. That means setting up briefings, lunches, news conferences, and private meetings for journalists. Journalists sometimes want to hear what the organ grinder has to say, not just listen to the monkey.

Be first

The trick is to make certain that the person the journalist deals with first is you, not the others. A good example is when, in February 1998, pharmaceutical company Smith Klein Beecham announced a possible merger with Glaxo Welcome. The merger was thought to have meant job losses, and the workers in question were represented by three different trade unions. Only one - MSF - was able to move quickly enough to get their General Secretary in front of cameras and on the radio on the Sunday when the story broke. Once MSF has established itself as the lead organisation in the debate standing up for the employees, the media returned to the MSF press office again and again, and the other unions were left out in the cold.

Get Quoted

If you can't be the initiator of a news story yourself, you can still get on the front page by being quoted in someone else's story. All news stories need quotes and comments, and if you can provide the snappy quote, it might well be used. If a news story demands a quote from an interested party responding to an event, there will be only one response, but perhaps scores of organisations and experts with a view on the matter.

For example, when the Government Green Paper on public health was published in early February 1998, Simon Buckby the *Financial Times'* social affairs correspondent had between fifteen and twenty organisations phoning and faxing to offer their response, but he would use only one. Here's how he explains the process: *'Faxes are best, when there's the story to write. I haven't the time to take calls. I'll look at the quote if it's catchy, novel, relevant. It doesn't have to be extreme. It can be an obvious view, but put in an interesting way. I need a straightforward 'Chairman of X organisation says...'. There needs to be a clear line. I don't need an eight page treatise when dealing with a news story.'*   After hundreds of people spent hours crafting thousands of words and attempting to get them to Simon, the final report contained a single quote, thirty words long, from one organisation.

If you can gain a reputation for providing a snappy quote and speedy reaction on your area of expertise to journalists, they'll keep coming back for more. MPs can wise up to this and get branded as 'rentaquotes'. You should keep your quotes short, so that words cannot be taken out of context, and your message isn't distorted or lost. If you are hamstrung by internal restrictions and clearance procedures, and waste three hours of the hack's time before offering a bland and inoffensive quote, the journalist (a) probably won't use it, and (b) won't ever phone you again.

Getting It Wrong
How to Annoy Journalists

Given the crowded market place for spin, journalists are constantly being phoned by people wanting to influence the news agenda. Often these calls are ill-conceived and wrongly-targeted, and serve only to annoy the journalist. Annoying journalists is not the way to get your message across.

As a stern warning, here is what a few of the thousands of journalists working in print and broadcast, have to say about their dealings with press officers, PRs and spin doctors:

1 Tim Lusher is editor of the daily Hot Tickets page of the *Evening Standard* (an events and 'what's on' guide). He works to daily tight deadlines, and comes under a barrage of faxed and posted news releases from record companies, clubs, band promoters, theatres, ballet companies, comedy venues and every other form of entertainment PR, all trying to get a slot on Tim's widely-read and influential page. A graduate in journalism from City University, he was a reporter on the *Western Morning News* for three years.

He says: *'The worst PRs are those who don't know who you are, and aren't sure what they're telling you or why. I don't mind PR people phoning to bounce ideas off me, but get annoyed when they clearly haven't read the page and offer material which is patently unsuitable.*

'The best PRs have all the information at their fingertips, and are ready with backup – photos, more information.

'A good news release is one which gets to the point straight away, and allows the reader to grasp the nettle immediately. They should be clear, concise and factual. If the intro is duff, the release will go straight in the bin. Journalists will speed-read a side of A4 in a few seconds before deciding whether it's worth pursuing.

'My advice to PRs is to research the market – read the paper you are targeting, watch the TV programme.'

2 Sally Shalam is the travel editor of the *Evening Standard*, and deals with press officers from airlines, tour operators, tourist boards and hotels. She has been in journalism for 15 years, and was previously a travel writer on the *Daily Telegraph*.

'We are inundated on a daily basis with news releases – between 25 and 50 each day. All are read by my deputy, some never reach me. We are always on the look out for anything which is different or quirky.

'Often news releases miss the story completely, or bury it down the page. I have to say the standard of releases has improved in the last couple of years.

'What drives me round the twist is press officers phoning to ask 'did you get my fax'. It shows no understanding of the workload or the amount of faxes we receive. Well-sussed PRs don't do it. You have to trust the fax machine to work! If we read all the faxes and answered all the calls, the Evening Standard's *travel pages would be blank!*

'My advice to PRs is to read the section of the paper they are targeting their press release at – a clever PR will know what a particular editor will pick up. PRs should spend some time in a real newsroom to see how it works and how busy it is.'

We rely heavily on PRs – we couldn't survive without them. The good ones provide an excellent service – they know their material and understand what we need.'

3 Lorraine Eames, 29, is a sub-editor on the evening daily *Bradford Telegraph and Argus*. She is a graduate of Sheffield School of Journalism and has been in journalism for three and a half years. Previously she worked as a reporter on the *Stockport Express*. As a local journalist, Lorraine's first question to people spinning her a story is always *'is it local?'*.

'As a reporter I dealt with around 30 press releases a day - most got put in the bin. The first thing to look for is if the release is about something local. I give news releases about ten seconds of attention before deciding whether to put it in the pile to read later.

'Sometimes releases would be about events in London, or five pages long - straight in the bin! I see releases which are too long, garbled, not clear, or worse - a good story sent too late for our deadline. PRs need to think of a good news angle, or something that will make a good picture, and often we'll use it.'

4 Mike Parkinson, 33, is the news editor on the *Hammersmith and Fulham Gazette*. He has been a West London-based journalist for ten years after graduating from the Harlow Centre for Journalism.

'I see between 10 and 15 news releases a day, and assess within five seconds whether I'm going to use it. I'm looking for a local angle - people who live or work in the local area, or services used by local people. Some releases are a right load of nonsense. I use about a third to a half of the stuff I'm sent.

'The worst recent example I've had is a ten minute spiel on the phone from a woman organising a charity event in Fulham (the area covered by Mike's paper). *When the fax arrived, it turned out the event was in Chelsea. It's frustrating to have your time wasted.'*

5 Dermot Kehoe, 30, worked as a researcher and producer for GMTV, including their 1997 General Election coverage and the *Sunday Programme*. During the election, he would be sent hundreds of news releases.

'I would read all releases briefly and quickly, but be on the look-out for either a strong story or a name. We need to put someone in front of the camera: a name like Henry Kissenger would catch the eye. The chief executive of some charity would not.

Dermot was on the receiving end of the political spin doctors during the election: *'Taking calls from spin doctors can be quite helpful. They can make your job easier by giving access to politicians and offering interview ideas - all subjected to rigorous scrutiny. Negotiating with spin doctors over interviews can be a buyers market or a sellers market. Sometimes, close to deadline, we are more desperate for interviewees to appear. Spin doctors have the ultimate sanction - to refuse to allow someone to appear. But it can be a hollow threat - they need TV too.'*

6 Simon Buckby, 31, is the social affairs correspondent for the *Financial Times*. His career in journalism includes stints as a producer for London Weekend Television including *'Walden'*, and reporter on BBC's *'On the Record'*.

'In a day, I get between one and a half and two inches of news releases and faxes in my in-tray - hundreds of pieces of paper. They fall into three categories: general stuff, which might not even be suited for a writer, it might be better for a local TV station; social affairs stuff aimed at all social affairs writers; and material aimed at me as a named individual. The danger is that the one you want gets lost with the rest.

'In a minute, I might deal with fifty pieces of paper. I read the headline, and maybe the first line. I look for organisations I know, but the story is the most important thing: it must be relevant and interesting.'

'Of unsolicited faxes and approaches, hardly any get used.

'Timing is important. There's no point phoning at 4.30pm when I've a 6.00pm deadline. Early mornings are best. There's no point phoning too far in advance either - about events two months away. You have to chose your moment.

'Journalists are not lazy, they are run off their feet. In a single day I might be writing two news stories, researching a feature, and digging around on a another story which might not even get in the paper.

'The best example is when they ring, but don't bug you. They phone on a Monday morning, and tell you about a press conference on the Tuesday. They fax through the details within five minutes, so its still fresh in your mind, with the information clear and not buried. Afterwards they phone to ask 'is there anything else', not to push a particular line. That's a dream.

'The worst is when they leave a message on the answerphone, just with a name and number, and ask you to call back, with no indication of where they are from. There might be ten a day, or more, and there isn't time to call them back.'

Journalists love to whinge about media relations people, except when they need information in a hurry or have to find a story with a deadline looming. Then they're on the phone being nice as pie. However, the kind of complaints listed above are all genuine, and show the dangers of getting it wrong.

Journalists can be devious too...

Journalists can be just as devious as spin doctors. The better the journalist, the more devious. Indeed the 'battle of wits' element of the job is what appeals to many on both sides of the news-creation process. A good journalist can use cajolery, flattery, bribery and threats just as effectively as a good spin doctor. Naturally, the public never read about slippery hacks up to no good in their newspapers, because it is the slippery hacks who write them. It is possible to be friendly with journalists, but never believe they can be your friends. You can take them into your confidence, but never completely trust them. There are plenty of powerful and savvy people who have let their guard down and lived to regret it.

It is not for nothing that journalists in American political argot are known as 'scorps' (short for scorpions). Like their deadly namesakes, scorps have plenty of sting in their tale. There are various tricks journalists can use to get information someone, somewhere, doesn't want them to know.

So be careful not to get stung....

Would you say that...

One of the oldest tricks in the book is the ascribing of quotes to individuals on the basis of a grunt of assent or a nod of the head. The scam runs as follows: the journalist says 'Would you say that the redundancies your firm is making will devastate the community?' You nod your head accepting you've heard the question and reply 'Yes, but in the medium term our £3 million retraining package will get people back to work.' Result? Headlines screaming 'DEVASTATION: firm predicts job loss chaos.'

I heard of a public relations consultant in the early stages of his career being tricked by a local paper over some client's misdemeanour. 'It's all been a bit of a cock-up, hasn't it?', suggested the hack. 'Well I suppose it must look like that, but the facts are...' replied our man. The local paper headline? One phrase, white out of black over half the front page: COCK-UP. This wasn't helped by the fact that the story concerned a local brewery, leading to the inevitable comments about organising a piss-up.

Be warned: anything a journalist says and you agree with, can be reported as your own view. The best way to avoid the 'wouldn't you say...' trap is to categorically deny the views expressed, and offer something else instead. If you simply deny the quote, you can be quoted as 'angrily rejecting allegations of corruption/sleaze/shop-lifting'.

The fictional Prime Minister, Francis Urquart's, way of dealing with it (if the journalist had got the right end of the stick) was to say 'You might say that, I couldn't possibly comment.' (and so another political catchphrase was born.)

The Pinter technique

In a normal conversation, a pause in the flow of conversation is deemed a social embarrassment, and the natural inclination for most people is to fill the silence with something, anything, usually the first thing that comes into your head. Journalists use this natural inclination to trick people into saying more than they intended, or to stray off-message.

It is important to remember that a broadcast interview, or a telephone call from a journalist is not a normal conversation, and the usual social rules of engagement are suspended.

Lengthy Pinter-esque silences from journalists are designed to make you blabber on and hopefully give something away. You should simply repeat your points over and over again. At a dinner party, endless repetition of the same point would be seen as a sign of crashing dullness or possibly mental instability. When dealing with journalists, it is a sign of professionalism and staying 'on-message.' Listen to Gordon Brown next time he's on the *Today* programme for an example of a maestro at work.

Wood for the trees

One trick is for the journalist to decide what information they want, and disguise their true intentions in a forest of other questions. Usually this takes the form of lengthy questions about the interviewee's area of expertise, designed to lull them into a false sense of security, and killer question is casually thrown in towards the end.

Early in her career, Lorna Fitzsimons, the Labour MP for Rochdale, blotted her otherwise impeccable copy-book with an interview in the *News of the World* in October 1997. During the course of a lengthy interview on her impressions of being a new MP, the role of the constituency representative, and her hopes for the future of Britain gave some astonishing quotes about sex. If you read the interview, you'll remember them.

Of course the *News of the World* only used the quotes about sex, ignored the dull but worthy mass of the interview, and Lorna Fitzsimons found herself the victim of a classic tabloid stitch-up. *'I may be an MP, but I need more sex'* ran the banner headline in the *News of the World's* glossy supplement, and the story ran on Monday in the anti-Labour *Telegraph* and *Mail*. In the wise words of *Guardian* journalist Julia Langdon, writing about the incident under a headline of *'Oh Dear'*: *'If you wish to discuss the serious side of your work as an MP, do not talk to the* News of the World.*'* Fair point.

The technique is not just used by tabloid hacks. The 'quality media' can be just as devious. I once gave an half-hour pre-recorded interview to *Newsnight* about the state of the Labour Party, all perfectly on-message, and towards the end was asked about the Tory defector Alan Howarth. I suggested it would be insane not to allow him to fight a Labour seat at the election (which he did, and now he is in the Government again). This controversial view, lasting ten seconds, was the only part that was broadcast, causing me untold grief with traditional members of the Labour Party for months, and the rest of the interview was left unbroadcast on the editing suite floor.

A variation on this approach is the **Columbo technique**: firing the killer question when your guard is down. Columbo, the seventies detective would lull his suspects into a false sense of security by acting like a bumbling dolt, and then deliver the killer question which tore apart the suspect's alibi with the preamble - *'there's just one thing bothering me...'*. Journalists use the same technique. While journalists can be friendly, they are never your friend.

I know your boss

This is a straightforward bluff where the hack implies they already know the information they are after, so that the press officer inadvertently gives the game away. It can usually work if the hack pretends to be best mates with your boss, or your bosses boss, and to have received the information first-hand.

I've fallen for this one. A journalist had heard a rumour that a Government Minister would be visiting their patch on 17th October, although this was a secret. He phoned me as the press officer dealing with the visit on the 16th September and said *'we're all ready for the Ministerial visit tomorrow...'* and I fell for it. Feeling rather pleased at the chance to make the hack look stupid, I replied *'you've got the wrong month, he's coming on 17th October'* and afterwards realised I had been tricked into releasing confidential information. Remember Gordon Jackson getting onto the train in the *Great Escape* being tricked into speaking English by the Gestapo, and always keep your guard up.

On-the-record/off-the-record

The difference between comments made 'off-the-record' or 'on-the-record' and non-attributable briefings need to be clearly understood. You should establish the ground rules before talking to a journalist, even in a social setting like lunch or over drinks. You should also be clear that what you mean by the term 'off-the-record' accords with what the hack thinks it means.

Off-the-record means that the information given will not be used. **Non-attributable** means that it may be used, but the source will not be revealed.

The non-attributable briefing is sometimes attached to a coded source such as 'Sources close to…' or 'Friends of so-and-so'. Sometimes no clue is given.

Most journalists are happy to play along with these rules, especially if you are a valued source of stories, but a useful rule of thumb is never say or reveal anything which you cannot afford to see repeated in print with you as the quoted source in tomorrow's newspapers.

As a result of the Labour Government's concern about the increase in 'off-message' stories appearing as a result of non-attributable briefings, Ministers have been warned to stay away from lunches with journalists without first checking with the spin control operation at Downing Street.

If in doubt, make it up...

Some journalists, in the absence of real information, simply make up quotes to back up their stories.

There, I've gone and said it.

Quotes can appear from 'sources close to…' or 'one backbencher said last night…' which could be anyone, and no one will ever know whether it was really said by a living person, or crafted by a harassed hack with a looming deadline. Stories about celebrities can be 'stood up' (given credibility) by quoting 'Friends of Piers Brosnan (or Jodie Foster or Madonna) said last night...' This formula is so vague as to be meaningless, and allows the journalist to write whatever they want.

Internal criticism from within an organisation can be invented, because no one will admit to it anyway, and quotes can usually be made up to substantiate stories about football transfers, Royal marriage rifts, and Cabinet rows. No one will ever know for sure.

Keep a Record

All of the above proves that when you are dealing with journalists you should always take notes of the conversation, and ask the journalist to read back what they've noted you as saying, to ensure that their understanding matches yours. You could even tape record the conversation – the chances are that the journalist is doing the same thing. If you're taping a phone conversation, you must tell the other person beforehand.

Journalists are professionals, trying to do a job in pressured situations. The tricks of the trade outlined above are considered sharp practice and techniques of good journalism. If you want to use the media and not the other way round, make sure you know the tricks they may try to pull.

4 Planning and Preparation

"The media is a large, complex organism, encapsulating hugely different types of organisations and individuals. You need to decide where you want to see your message appear, and plan accordingly."

Spin doctoring must be planned out in advance. You must decide what messages you want to get across, to whom, using what methods and resources, and you must decide the best time to do it. But before you do any of that you must be clear *why* you want to do it.

It might be because you want more people to come to visit your restaurant, or buy your cornflakes, or vote for you in the council elections. It might be because you want to get noticed within your firm or organisation. It might be because you want people to be saying certain things about you. You might want to walk into your local pub and have people say, 'saw your picture in the paper'. It might even be that you want to become a household name. Whatever the reason, you must be clear why you are spinning. Once you know why you are doing it, you need to answer the following questions:

What's the context?

Before you start, you need to find out what your environment is. In commercial spin doctoring, that means conducting extensive opinion polling, market research, focus groups, product testing, and surveys.

In politics it means gathering every fact and figure on your opponent's record, and recording every statement and article to expose inconsistencies and gaffes. At Labour's election HQ at Millbank, London, the technique was mastered using a database called Excaliber

(Excaliber was the sword of truth in Arthurian legend), which documented everything ever said or done by every Tory candidate, and used against them to great effect.

You have to be aware of the climate in which you are operating - what the are the **S**trengths, **W**eaknesses, **O**pportunities and **T**hreats. Creating a SWOT analysis, listing points under the separate headings, helps clarify your thinking. You should be aware of what the opposition are doing and saying. Even at low-levels, you need to work out what obstacles there are to successful spin doctoring. If you want to get your article on hang-gliding into your company staff newsletter to impress the Chief Executive, make sure they didn't carry an article on that subject last week, or that the Chief Executive's wife hasn't just broken her legs in a hang-gliding accident.

What's the message?

What is it you want to say? There is a maxim that all advertising must contain a truth - that Volvos are safe, that eggs are good for you, that the *Sun* is fun. They used to sell cigarettes by telling you doctors smoked them, or they were good for your throat. Now, in the light of medical evidence, no one would believe it, so they sell cigarettes on the basis of lifestyle and image. Recent ad campaigns have attempted to tell us that meat and sugar are healthy, despite evidence to the contrary. The ad campaigns that work are ones which tell us something we already believe, or want to believe. The same is true of spin doctoring. The message you want to get across must have, at its heart, a truth - something that people will believe. All the spin doctoring in the world cannot sell a message that no one believes.

The Herculean efforts by spin doctors to make Labour leader Neil Kinnock a plausible candidate for Prime Minister - constraining his natural ebullience and sense of humour, filling his speeches with econobabble - all counted for nought, because in the end, despite millions preferring him to Thatcher and Major, not enough voters believed in him.

So your message must be **believable**, or one which people want to believe. It must contain enough truth to pass the plausibility test. The whole of Labour's 1997 election campaign was based on this principle. The promises made (the Five Pledges) were seen as modest and straightforward, and repeated by every candidate and spokesman until we were saying them in our sleep. Some people attacked the pledges for being too timid, but no one could accuse Labour of making promises it couldn't deliver.

Staying on message

The message must be repeated and repeated. If you say something a thousand times, on the thousandth time someone, somewhere, is hearing it fresh. The people who are hearing it for a second or third time are having the message reinforced. It is also important to stay 'on message'. This means that if you stray from what you originally said, people might spot the discrepancy and expose you. Within an organisation it means that if the chief executive says, for example, that next year will be a successful one for the company, then everyone else from the Head of Sales to the lift attendant should be saying the same thing.

Japanese companies will spend weeks training lift-attendants, receptionists and chauffeurs, not in their actual jobs, but in how to present the company to outsiders. A visitor to a corporation will spend their first vital few minutes of contact, not with a senior executive or smooth PR man, but with the receptionist or lift attendant. In Japan, they can give you facts, figures, and spin about the company, whereas in the UK the likelihood is you'll get a surly temp or empty-headed bimbo. In some organisations you'll be lucky if they even acknowledge your presence.

Once you've decided 'the line' you must stay 'on message'.

Who do I want to hear it?

The key concept in spin doctoring is that there is no such thing as 'the public'. There are, instead, a series of 'publics' who have to be dealt with differently. You have to decide who your 'target audience' is and communicate with them accordingly. This judgement is one of the most important you will make: your target might be millions of people, or it might be just one person. Who do you want to hear your message? People as voters, consumers, or investors? People within your organisation? Your opponents? Your boss?

The idea of different 'publics' comes from marketing and advertising. In advertising campaigns, the target audiences can number millions - for example all females aged 16-24 in social class ABC1. Advertisers and marketing men segment the potential markets for their products in all kinds of different ways. Here are the main ones.

Demographics (age, sex, stage of life cycle, etc.) A target audience for a pensions company might be all women and men over 50. And the target for a new women's magazine might be all women aged 16-24.

Socio-economics For example, the National Readership Survey categories of A, B, C1, C2, D, E, in which A equals higher managerial, administrative or professional people, and E equals pensioners, casuals, and the unemployed. These are broad, sweeping categories, and there are exceptions (for example lottery winners and premiership footballers), but some products may be targeted at managers rather than the unemployed.

Geo-demographics Where social class is cross referenced with geographical location using systems like ACORN, Pinpoint and Mosaic. Certain postcodes imply status or wealth, such as SW6, and so those people are more likely to be interested in luxury goods. Postcodes which cover areas with high crime rates might be good for selling car alarms or security systems.

Lifestyle (how when, why and on what people spent their money). Some people prefer to buy things by mail-order, some take holidays abroad, some are interested in alternative lifestyles, etc.,

Psycho-graphics The study of attitudes, interests and opinions of people. If someone gives money to an animal welfare charity, they may consider donating to other good causes.

Advertising and marketing is becoming increasingly sophisticated, so that direct mail can pinpoint particular types of consumer. The admen can find out a great deal of information about all of us. Millions of pounds are spent on lists of consumers. A list of those who buy wine from a mail-order wine club, is worth investigating by a company which sells luxury foods by mail-order. A list of people who eat in restaurants once a week is valuable to the owners of a new restaurant.

In an election campaign the target audiences might be broken down into particular social classes 'C2's', 'Essex Man' or 'Worcester Women', on the basis of how they voted last time and how they intend to vote this time ('Tory switchers' and 'Lib Dem waverers') and even at the level of target seats, towns, wards and streets.

In spin doctoring, the market segment can number from the millions to a 'segment of one' (an individual). For example, in the eighties, Tory ministers would fight like dogs to appear on the *Today Programme* at a certain time. Why? Because they knew that *Today* was one of the few programmes their leader Margaret Thatcher listened to. She was the one person who could hire or fire them, and they wanted to reach her via the airwaves.

Only when you know with whom you wish to communicate, can you make decisions on how and where.

What types of media should I employ?

As we have seen, the media is a large, complex organism, encapsulating hugely different types of organisations and individuals. You need to decide where you want to see your message appear, and plan accordingly. If you want to reach corporate decision-makers, you might want to target the *Financial Times*, the *Economist, Management Today, Investors Chronicle* or the finance sections of the *Times* and *Telegraph*. But there would be little point trying to get your story in the *Sun* or the *Mirror,* or on day-time TV.

The best way is to draw up a target list of media, and decide how to approach each of them one by one. You need to do some research. This might include reading newspapers and magazines to get an idea of the kinds of stories they print, looking out for the by-lines of journalists who write about subjects in your field, or the names of specialist correspondents. It might include listening and watching broadcasters to deconstruct their programmes and spot opportunities.

Drawing up your target list can be made easier by using publications which list all the media in the UK, with their contact details.

- *Benns Media Directory* is a large directory of all UK and over 30,000 international titles.

- The *Guardian Media Guide* is an annual handbook, including lists and information.

- *Pims* and *Editors* are regularly updated media lists covering all national, local, trade and technical publications and all radio and television. Subscribers are sent automatic updates, to take account of the shifting sands of the media.

From your understanding of the media, you should begin to pick apart the components of your story, and tailor it to different types of media. Every story can be viewed from different angles, and has different layers.

For example, a syndicate of local government workers win £2 million on the National Lottery. There are a number of different angles, and different media outlets. On the surface the story is a national news story - the tabloids will be interested to carry the story as a straight piece of feel-good news. The syndicate worked in local government - so the story might provide a little light relief in a serious trade magazine such as Local *Government Chronicle* or *Municipal Journal*. The winners all live somewhere - so the local papers, radio and TV will want to cover the story from a local angle. The in-house journal of the council will want to cover the story, as would the magazine of the winners' trade union UNISON. There might even be follow-up media opportunities such as features on what is like to win the lottery, and a good magazine journalist might revisit the winners after a year to write a feature about how they dealt with being suddenly rich.

One of the journalists' most common complaints is that of having their time wasted by a spin doctor who is simply contacting the wrong person. Radio stations get sent photographs, the *Manchester Evening News* is faxed a release about a story in Leicester, the health correspondent is sent a release about a new library. This is a waste of everyone's time, effort and money which is why targeting is so important.

What methods shall I use?

As we shall see later in the book, there are a variety of methods to use, from sending out hundreds of news releases and staging major media conferences, to off-the-record briefings and letters to the local paper. You need to decide the most efficient and cost-effective method. The most unimaginative, nuts-and-bolts approach, as used by many PR agencies, is the scatter-gun approach where hundreds of news releases are sent out in the hope that some will find the target. Most fall on stony ground. More sophisticated methods draw on highly tailored approaches to particular types of media, based on a thorough understanding of their priorities and tastes, and even approaches to individual journalists based on an existing relationship.

You should never forget that there is more to spin doctoring than straightforward news. Using features, letters to the editor, photos, book-reviews and profiles can aid your cause just as effectively as screaming headlines.

When will I do it, and how much will it cost?

Timing can be crucial. You can make good use of times when news is slack, such as the silly season in August, and on New Years Day. A call to a newsroom of a daily paper on a Sunday morning is always appreciated, as the reporters are looking to fill the Monday edition. You need to work out a plan of action, with week-by-week targets, but you should build in flexibility. Often you can't predict with accuracy what the media will do with a particular story, and when an opportunity arises you have to run with it, but having a game plan at least at the outset is a good start.

You need to keep some sort of budget in mind. Spin doctoring is open-ended. You could spend millions on massive mail-outs, photography, celebrity endorsements, video news releases, stunts, satellite link-ups and expensive freebies to Fiji. Or you might just make a few phone-calls.

How do I know if I have been successful?

Spin doctoring is an imprecise activity – it's difficult to measure in any scientific way. You can set obvious strategic goals – such as avoiding a corporate take-over, sending a book to the best-seller lists, winning an election.

At its most crude, evaluation can be simply measuring the number of column inches in the press and the number of minutes of airtime and adding them up month by month. But that doesn't take any account of the impact of the coverage, the number of readers, the treatment in the editorial, or the positive or negative angle taken. Public relations firms and in-house teams monitor the media and track messages against agreed criteria, like position on the page, size of headline and so on.

One way of impressing clients is to ascribe the results of spin doctoring with an advertising equivalent rate – so that an item covering four column inches in the *Sun* would be valued at the cost of buying the same amount of space in the *Sun* as advertising. This is, however, slightly disingenuous as advertising rates are very high, and editorial is treated differently by readers from advertising).

There are several companies which specialise in media monitoring, and can supply you with press cuttings from across the UK, and tapes of broadcasts, based on keywords and subjects which you give them. For example Durrants Press Cuttings Limited, CXT Limited and Romeike and Curtice can supply press cuttings. The Press Express service from Romeike and Curtice can supply daily clippings by 8am.

On radio and television, the Broadcast Monitoring Company and Parker Bishop can supply audio tapes, videos, summaries and transcripts of programmes.

No matter how broad or narrow your goals, you should set out some targets in advance against which to measure your success, and learn from your failures.

Contacts
Spin doctoring is a contact sport

Contacts are the spin doctors life-blood. Spinning to a journalist with whom you have an on-going relationship based on trust is much more likely to be successful than a 'cold call' to an unknown journalist. The spin doctor should nurture contacts with journalists, offer help and advice, give them occasional favours and special treatment, but always be prepared to challenge them, and complain to their editors.

Most of the time, your contact with journalists will be on the telephone. There are not many stories in the journalists busy day that cannot be handled with a phone call and a fax of extra information or news release.

If your contact with the journalist is likely to be on-going, you might suggest a drink or lunch, or to meet up at a conference or event at which you will both be present. If you do, it is a good idea to have some gossip or story ideas up your sleeve to make the hack feel that the time has not been wasted.

Every time you speak to a journalist, you should log the call and make a record of their details. In co-ordinated PR campaigns, the frequency of calls from certain journalists can be a useful indicator of progress.

Building up your list of contacts, and keeping the contact fresh is a hugely valuable investment to make. If your contact is not someone you bump into on the social or professional circuit, you should work at keeping the contact 'hot'. You can use the sending of Christmas cards as a way of reminding people where you are. You should also send 'new job' cards when you move jobs, so that your contacts do not lose touch.

A good contact-builder will phone every few months for a chat, or on some spurious piece of business, to keep the contact alive. Suggest lunch, or a 'swift half' after work. Most people like being phoned out of the blue and invited out by someone they haven't seen for a while, and if they don't, they'll soon make it obvious. It is possible to keep contacts for decades, on the basis of a phone-call three times a year.

Most successful people are good at building contacts. Some people can remember names of people in hundreds of organisations going back for years. Harold Wilson was supposed to be able to remember the name of everyone he ever met. Bill Clinton maintained card-index files in shoeboxes on every useful person he met from his college days onwards, until he became President of the United States.

His biographer Martin Walker claims '*There was never a more assiduous maintainer of acquaintance and friendship than Clinton, and his political network was extraordinary...names, addresses, phone numbers and birthdays, weddings and children, updated with new jobs and the latest publications, new meetings and family bereavements, they were all cross referenced, with a note of any campaign contributions they had made.*' When the cards were finally transferred onto computer, there were more than 10,000 files.

The importance of having 'contacts' can be overplayed. If your story is strong enough, and if you have something journalists want, it won't matter if you've never spoken before. Similarly, if your story is ropey, a journalist will not write it up simply because you bought them lunch. However, if a journalist needs a quote from a particular viewpoint, and there are a number of people and organisations capable of supplying the quote, the journalists will go for the one he or she knows best, and can be trusted to come up with a decent punchy quote on the spot.

The contacts book is probably the most important tool of the trade. Tales abound of panic-stricken spin doctors who have realised their Filofax has been stolen, or the power supply on their Psion organiser has failed and all data lost. The lesson of these disaster stories is to back-up everything on computer, or photocopy all pages of the Filofax or contacts book. You have been warned.

5 Spinning in Print

*"Given how many millions of news releases are produced
and pumped out by press offices every year, it is amazing
how many are totally rubbish: badly written,
wrongly targeted, and destined for the waste bin."*

The News Release
In the news or in the bin?

The News Release is still the basic tool of the spin doctor (it should always be called a news release not press release, as this excludes broadcasters). It is one or two-sided document sent from an organisation to a journalist containing a new story, or occasionally useful information. The news release is designed to whet a journalist's appetite for more.

At the advanced stages of spin doctoring, it becomes unnecessary, when a phone-call, a tip-off, or in the case of Peter Mandelson even a slightly-raised eyebrow, can make the news. (Peter's awesome reputation must become something of a nuisance at times, when his every nuance and movement is scrutinised for hidden meaning. It reminds me of the story of French Statesman, Charles Maurice de Talleyrand. On hearing of the death of Austrian Statesman, Klemens Metternich, he commented, *'I wonder what he meant by that?'*)

Given how many millions of news releases are produced and pumped out by press offices every year, it is amazing how many are totally rubbish: badly written, wrongly targeted, and destined for the waste bin.

Talk to any journalist and they will tell you the huge proportion of news releases which never get read beyond the first paragraph. Some news releases - addressed to journalists who have died, or to magazines which have gone out of business, or offering photo-opportunities to Red Rose Radio, Preston, don't even get read.

But news releases can be successful, with some thought, skill and effort, and if they follow the rules of engagement.

Producing a news release is like making a cake. Even with the right ingredients, if they are mixed wrongly, the result is a real mess. And if the cake is made correctly, but served as a starter or to someone allergic to cake mix, it is a failure.

Like cake, a news release must have the right ingredients, be mixed in the right order, delivered at the right time, and to the right people. Even then, good fortune plays a part. You might have a great story about a new type of bicycle chain and issue it on the day war is declared with China.

News releases must be high-quality, eye-catching, and interesting to the journalist.

A news release is geared solely at one audience: the journalist. It has only one purpose: to get the organisation's core messages to target audiences via the media.

The issuing of news releases is not a performance indicator nor the end product of media relations - merely a means to an end.

The curse of poor spin doctoring, as practised by useless PR people, is to produce news releases which are aimed at pleasing the client. This is the spin doctors' equivalent of Going on the Game.

These news releases are characterised by fulsome praise of the client's organisation or product, positioning the client's name in the headline and opening sentence, and splattering the copy with superlatives. (For example, it is unlikely that any senior manager of any company in Britain is capable of making an 'epoch-making speech to shareholders' or that any new design of screwdriver is 'revolutionary').

This kind of public relations prostitution serves to

✗   give real spin doctors a bad name

✗   annoy the pants off journalists, and

✗   fail to make any impact whatever on the media.

✗   It is also a sad reflection on the empty lives of senior managers that they get a boost to their egos by seeing their names on press releases – written by people on their own pay-role.

Whilst there are no hard and fast rules on whether to issue a release, or use another method, it is usual to use a news release for a "broadcast" announcement to a wide spread of media. A more targeted approach such as a phone-call should be used for an 'exclusive' or a story more specific to one particular publication.

Here are some pointers on format and style for news releases.

News Release Format

The format must be consistent and meet journalists' expectations of the information they need. News journalists receive hundreds of news releases every day, and can spare just a few seconds in deciding whether to read them or not. The format for news releases must therefore follow the accepted rules of journalism and transmit the necessary information quickly. Obeying these rules of format and structure is the best way to stand a decent chance of your release being read.

Paper and spacing

News releases should be produced on news release printed paper, single-sided, with a special continuation sheet. They are produced in 12 point in 1.5 or 2 line spacing, aligned left, with wide margins, perhaps 2.5cm (1") left and right margins and a 2.5cm top and bottom margin.

Wide margins and spacing allow the sub-editors to scribble all over your news release. The release must always be on a single side of paper because journalists will not bother to turn over the page. The top of the release usually has a company or organisation name and logo for swift identification. Journalists will look first to see who is issuing the release, and assess their importance. Larger organisations will put an identification code here, to track their releases. This might be the number and year, like this: PR004/98. This might go at the end of the release. Also, at the top of the release should appear the words 'news release'. This may seem like over-egging the pudding, but it is part of the process of supplying the information in a quickly accessible form for journalists who are dealing with myriad sources of information.

Date or embargo?

At the top left comes the date on which the news is issued, or the date and time of the embargo that you wish to place on the information contained in the release. Embargoes are used to warn journalists that information issued in advance of an event or announcement cannot be published or transmitted to the public. It is usual for journalists to observe this convention, but if a journalist feels that they can scoop their rivals, and if the source is unimportant enough to risk annoying, they may break the embargo for the sake of the story.

The convention for news embargoed to a specific day is

EMBARGO: 00.01hrs Monday Xxth June 1998

i.e one minute past midnight on the day of release. This enables news-papers to write the story the day before for appearance on the nation's breakfast tables the following morning. Such an embargo would also allow overnight radio and TV news bulletins and morning radio and TV news to broadcast the story.

Contact details

Contact details should appear at the top as well as at the end of a news release and include the name of the person journalists should phone and their contact numbers for 24 hours. This is to make the process of follow-up as easy as possible for the journalist, and to ensure that if the news release follows onto a second side, the contact details are not separated and lost.

It is important that the details are correct, and that the person named has not just gone on holiday. If the named contact intends to be away from the phone, they should brief a colleague so that the call from a journalist is not lost. Ideally the spin doctor should have a mobile and a pager so that journalists can reach them 24 hours a day.

News is a continuous process, and reporters may well be working on a story late at night, on a Sunday for the Monday editions, and bids for interview may come in early in the morning. Indeed Sunday is a busy day for spin doctors and journalists, preparing for the Monday editions and programmes. Spin doctoring is no nine-to-five occupation.

For attention of...

Below the contact details comes where in the media organisation the news release is directed. So: "for the attention of housing correspondents" or "for newsdesks" or "for the attention of forward planning desks". This helps get the news release in the right person's hands quickly. If you are not sure who the release should be aimed at, put 'for newsdesks'. It is always best, if possible, to put the name of the actual journalist who will cover the story, which is where building up contacts and researching your market becomes essential.

Operational Note

Occasionally the news release will not contain news, but information relevant to the operations of a newsroom. For example, that a press officer's home 'phone number has changed, or that a media event's venue has been moved. In these cases, OPERATIONAL NOTE is written above the heading, upper case, aligned left.

Notice of photo-opportunity

If the news release is an invitation to photographers (or 'snappers' in the vernacular) to attend a photo-opportunity, type NOTICE OF PHOTO-OPPORTUNITY above the heading.

Heading

The heading is bold, centred, usually upper-case, and a maximum of three lines deep (a triple-decker). This is one element of the release which will almost always be read.

Body text

The body text is the main chunk of text on a news release. It is perhaps 12 point Times (the font) aligned left, arranged in short paragraphs, without sub-headings.

More follows or ends

The bottom of the first page must inform the journalist whether there is more on a following page (in which case write "more follows..." aligned right, lower case at the bottom of the page). If the body text has come to an end, let the journalist know: write "ends" aligned left, lower case.

Slug or catchline

At the top of a continuation sheet comes the 'catchline' or "slug" - telling the journalist that the page is a continuation and identifying the story. The slug is upper case and preceded by a forward slash, and should reflect the story. So, the first thing on the second page of a news release about youth crime would be /CRIME2, on the third page /CRIME3, etc.

Notes to editors

Notes to editors is a convention whereby extra background information is supplied to journalists. These are numbered, and the first note will always be the same: the explanation of what the organisation is and what it does.

The second note might be information about a spokesperson being available for interview, or that a publication is available on request.

Finally, the news release must end with a contact for more information, with 24-hour contact numbers, including home and mobile numbers.

All of the above advice is just guidance – not all news releases coming into a newsroom look identical. But you should try to make all your organisation's news releases follow the same rules, so that journalists feel comfortable with them and know they will contain the information they need. News releases are designed to spoon-feed busy journalists and encourage them to use the information you have sent them. If the news release is difficult to read or if the story is unclear, you have failed.

Style and Structure

News releases must contain news. This may seem an obvious statement, but this the test which most news releases fail dismally. Your release may not be announcing the new Pope, but it must contain something newsworthy to the journalist reading it. News releases must be written in the same style as newspaper news stories, obeying the same rules, and avoiding any confusion with other styles of documents such as reports or memos.

Finding the strongest news-angle is part of the skill of the spin doctor, and as we have seen, 'news' can be a variety of different treatments of the same set of facts.

Structure

There is an established convention on the structure of a news release, which mirrors the way journalists are trained to write news stories. If you can write close to the style of the publication you are targeting, the journalist will feel comfortable with your material.

Firstly, you need a good headline. When a journalist receives your release, they will scan the organisation's name, the headline, and perhaps the first paragraph, in under ten seconds. Your headline must be attractive and tell the story. Look at the way newspapers use headlines to draw the reader into the story, and attempt to emulate the style.

The first paragraph contains the "intro." of the story (or "nose" in USA, or "L'Attaque" in France) - and contains the famous five W's of the story:

⇨ Who,

⇨ What,

⇨ Where,

⇨ When, and

⇨ Why.

These are the key components of the story, and they must all be there.

The first paragraph encapsulates the whole story and entices the journalist to read on by concentrating on the most news-worthy element of the story (the "angle" or "peg".) From the five W's, the strongest angle might be just "where" and "what". "Where" is particularly relevant for local newspaper journalists who want to ascertain quickly whether the story concerns their patch. If the story is about a celebrity, then 'who' is the best angle. If the story is about an usual event or stunt, then you would lead on 'what'. As your news release writing becomes more confident, you can try different ways of using the five W's.

For most organisations the strongest angle is seldom "who", which is why news releases must start with something more newsworthy than "X Organisation today announced...". That may be what the organisation wants to hear, but it isn't what will excite a news reporter.

The first paragraph should be short and snappy. The first sentence should be no longer than 30 words. Read the opening paragraphs of newspaper reports to see the technique in practice. Here's an example of an intro. from the Department of the Environment, Transport and the Regions (DETR) dated 5th November 1997:

Environment Minister, Michael Meacher (who) yesterday (when) visited Washington (where) for key talks (what) on climate change (why) with the Clinton administration.

Or this from the Consumers Association on 3rd February 1998:

Airport capacity (what) is at breaking point due to the failure of past governments to address the problem (why), according to an article in Consumer Policy Review (who) published today (when).

Subsequent paragraphs should expand on aspects of the five W's, with less important information and quotes coming further down the text.

Quotations should be as short and punchy as possible. Nothing crucial to the story should be buried in latter stages of the body text. Journalists often complain that something worthwhile and interesting has been buried in the fifth paragraph after 200 words of corporate-speak or jargon.

News releases should never be longer than two pages, and in most cases should on one page. If you can't tell the story in less than two sides, you need to rethink the bare bones of the story. Remember the point of a news release is to attract attention in a hugely competitive market, not be a comprehensive document. If the journalist needs more information than is contained in the release, they will phone you. There is nothing worse than a four or five page news release: you may as well not bother and go to the pub instead.

Clearing news releases

Organisations need a clearance procedure for news releases. This is a necessary process to ensure the release is not incorrect in the technical details, illegal, or untrue. It also provides a second opinion, and to be honest, covers the back of the spin doctor if something goes wrong.

If a news release is issued with incorrect data or a mistake, it is conventional for a second release to be issued, putting right the mistake. This is a real pain in the neck, and can be avoided by getting it right first time.

The clearance process should be as speedy as possible. If the release mentions or quotes other organisations, they should clear it as well. It is important for the people who are clearing the release to realise that they are checking for factual errors, not altering style. Journalists will not hang around while six different people meddle with your news release.

At English Partnerships, the soon-to-be-abolished government quango responsible for doling out regeneration cash, I wrote a news release which ended up being cleared by eight different people, including the

Chief Executive, the Company Secretary, the Head of Communications, the technical expert dealing with the case, and the Regional Secretary for the area where the story was taking place. I might as well have shown it to the cleaners and the cat. By the time (ten hours later) the release was finally cleared and issued, all the journalists were in the pub or with their wives and children. No wonder you haven't ever heard of English Partnerships.

A means NOT an end

A news release is a means not an end. It is a method of alerting a journalist to a story, of selling the story you are offering in competition with all the other people selling stories. That's why it must have the right combination of clear and recognisable format, coupled with a strong, well-written story. News releases are not easy documents to craft, despite the surprising number of people who think they can rattle them off in a few minutes. That is why the ratio of news releases issued to those used is roughly the same as the survival rate of lemmings.

News Releases Checklist

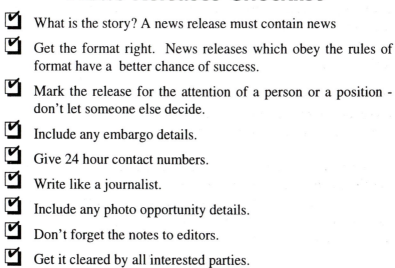

☑ What is the story? A news release must contain news

☑ Get the format right. News releases which obey the rules of format have a better chance of success.

☑ Mark the release for the attention of a person or a position - don't let someone else decide.

☑ Include any embargo details.

☑ Give 24 hour contact numbers.

☑ Write like a journalist.

☑ Include any photo opportunity details.

☑ Don't forget the notes to editors.

☑ Get it cleared by all interested parties.

☑ Follow it up - but don't pester.

☑ Remember, news releases are a means, not an end. There may be better means.

Feature Writing

Feature articles are the longer articles carried by newspapers and magazines. They are usually related to an aspect of the news or current events, and allow the publication to explore an issue in greater depth, with more content and opinion, and often from a controversial or unusual angle. In most publications they are written by non-staff contributors, allowing a range of experts, freelances, and the 'great and the good' to appear.

Subject matter can cover virtually anything, from serious 'think pieces' about the Asian tiger economies in the *Financial Times,* to detailed articles about the technicalities of local government finance in *Municipal Journal*, to light and fluffy articles about ce-lebrities' kitchens in *Hello*.

A story in the news can spark a rash of features. Clare Short is reunited with the son she gave up for adoption - and there are endless features about adoption. Jack Straw's son is set up for possession of cannabis, and there are acres of coverage about drug use.

Anniversaries and events can be the peg for feature articles. In early January, there are always articles about giving up smoking, or dieting, or keeping new year resolutions. To be controversial, the *Daily Telegraph* chose 2nd January 1998 to carry an article by Emily Mortimer in support of cigarette smoking (*'Why I won't give up the joy of smoking'*). Every summer, expect features on skin cancer and drought. And every winter expect features on drink driving and attempts to an-swer the question 'has Christmas become too commercial?'

There are other numerous 'diary dates' which different types of journalist plan their year around, from company's financial results, the start of the football season, solar eclipses, and the London Marathon, to No Smoking Day, International Women's Day and the party political conferences.

There are two ways of using features. One is to do it yourself, and use the opportunity to profile your boss in a feature under their own by-line. The second is to persuade a journalist to take up your issue or campaign, and for them to write it and sell it.

Persuading a journalist to write a feature is high-risk, because you lose control over what is written, but has the advantage of credibility because it is written by an independent third-party.

Doing it yourself

Many local papers have a 'Soap box' or 'Your Shout' feature where readers with a strong view are invited to submit articles. Often these slots are high-jacked by professional campaigners, but the editors prefer 'real' people with a gripe about a local issue. For example the *Hammersmith Gazette* has recently carried features from local people on everything from fluoride in the water to the BSE crisis.

Spin doctors are responsible for 'ghosting' articles for their masters. Politicians usually do not have the time nor talent to knock out 300 word articles for tabloids on tackling crime, or education standards, so the task is given to their spin doctors. One of Alastair Campbell's contributions to the projection of Tony Blair is the regular flow of articles in the *Sun, Mirror, Mail* and *Express*.

An article under the by-line of a Chief Executive or Company Chairman appearing in Management Today, the Director or a relevant trade magazine allows him to demonstrate leadership, display expertise, and perhaps plug his company's services or products.

Feature articles' structure and style

Features allow a greater variety of structures and styles than straight news reporting. There is less pressure to start the article in with the 'five-W's' formula. The intro. can use different devices to draw the reader into the article.

You can set up a question to engage the reader such as this feature from *Country Life,* September 1995: *'When did you last see, or hear, a skylark?'* or this from the football mag *Four Four Two: 'How good is Rio Ferdinand?'* Try a teaser, such as this intro., again from *Country Life: 'Duff House is a thrilling building, made all the more so by its unlikely situation.'*

You can start with a historical reference point, such as this intro. from an article about St Helena in *New Statesman* (2 Jan 1998): *'St Helena enjoys one great claim to fame - as the place where Napoleon was banished and lived the last six years of his life in exile.'*

You can aim to shock the reader, as Julie Burchill does in an article in the *Modern Review* (November 1997) calling for censorship of exploitative images of children: *'There has never been a better time to be a child-molester.'*

Features about people or interviews might start with a single characteristic. In *George*, (January 1997) the American political mag, John Kennedy opened his interview with an ABC news reporter with the line: *'The first thing you notice about Cokie Roberts, in real life, is her eyes...'*

'New Lad' magazines can use humour, such as this from December 1997's FHM: *'However boring your girlfriend is in bed, you only have to turn on a wildlife documentary to see that there are plenty of other creatures who have a much worse sex life than you.'*

Or you can try a straightforward scene-setter like this article in February 1998's *GQ* magazine about Newcastle United star Malcolm Macdonald: *'The grey concrete and steel stands of St James's Park steeple up from a hilltop overlooking Newcastle, visible from every direction, like a modern cathedral calling the citizenry to worship.'*

There are endless varieties of intros, and with practice, you should deploy different ways of hooking the reader into your article.

Selling in the article

The key target journalist is the Features Editor, who edits the features section, plans the schedule of features, commissions writers, and manages in-house feature writers. This person also has the rotten job of being the target of every genuine freelance, spin doctor, and amateur who thought they'd have a go at writing an article about their trip to Corfu. This means they are every bit as harassed by phone-calls, unsolicited articles and faxes, as news reporters. They appreciate being dealt with in a professional manner.

Before writing an article you should research your market. Read your target publications carefully. Decide what kind of articles have been published before. Look at the content, length, tone and style, and emulate it. Write an article which you could easily imagine appearing in your chosen target. Getting your article published is known as 'placing' your article. You can send in your finished article totally unsolicited ('on spec') to the features editor, but this is unlikely to be successful. It is possible (I have had a couple of articles in the *Guardian* which were submitted on spec), but a much better way is to seek agreement from the features editor in advance. You should discuss your idea, perhaps with a brief synopsis, with the features editor, and if they like the idea they will commission you to write the article.

It is usual for non-staff contributors to feature pages to be paid, unlike contributors to news pages. The fee should be agreed in advance. Usually there is a standard rate for the job , based in number of words or 'lineage' (number of lines). There could be a 'kill fee' - a payment paid for a commissioned article which isn't actually published. For working freelance journalists, the point of getting feature articles published is to pay the bills and stop their house contents being repossessed. For the spin doctor, the point is profile-building or opinion-moulding.

This means that the issue of payment is very different for journalists than spin doctors. My view is that when spin doctors offer feature material, they should insist on the going rate for the job. That means the vast PR industry isn't doing journalists out of work, and forcing contribution fees down. You can either keep the cash or give it to charity - its the principle that counts. On the other hand, on smaller publications, the fact that spin doctors can offer features without requiring payment gives them the edge over other, competing contributors, and might mean the article is more likely to be published. Let your conscience decide.

Feature article checklist

- ☑ Research your market and judge the features editor's tastes
- ☑ Try to get a commission, rather than submitting the article on spec
- ☑ Use different devices such as teasers, historical context, questions and scene-setters to open your article
- ☑ Redraft until you're happy with the result

Other Types of Article

Book reviews

Most publications carry reviews of forthcoming books, especially in the trade and technical sector, and reviews can be a good way of getting profile. Publications will have a designated Reviews Editor, who is inundated with review copies of books from publishing houses. These are sent free in the hope that publications will review them, and the book will receive some publicity. Reviews editors choose their reviewers with care, and try to match the book to the reviewer in a way that will make interesting copy. A biography of a famous politician might be reviewed by another politician who knew him or her well; perhaps even their sworn enemy. Either way, the review will have a sharpness and relevance.

Sometimes established or celebrity reviewers can use the review article almost as a comment piece - using the publication of a new book about cricket to write 300 words on the parlous state of English cricket, or the latest edition of Dodds to have a rant about the aristocracy.

If you or your boss are attempting to build a profile as a thinker or authority in a particular area, then reviewing books can help establish a reputation. You can phone publishing houses and ask the public relations or marketing section for 'review copies' of books, although they will ask for proof of a commission to write a review, or examples of past reviews.

Obituaries

The articles summing up a noted or famous person's life and activities when they die. National newspapers have obituaries already written for everyone in public life, which are updated regularly. Sometimes, as well as the official obituary, shorter obits can appear by people who knew the person well at a particular time or in a particular field. These can be very personal memories or comments, sometimes simply an anecdote which encapsulated the deceased's personality. Obituaries can be submitted to the obituary editor, and can be a fitting way to pay tribute to a respected figure.

Profiles

The longer articles about a single person, usually a celebrity, and often based on an interview. They tend to appear when celebs have a new book or film to plug. If you or the person you are spinning for gets the opportunity to be the subject of a profile, jump at it. You might even phone the journalist whose name appears under profiles and suggest they profile you, if you feel interesting enough. These features, always accompanied by a photograph, are the sign that you've arrived, even if it is just in the local paper or trade mag. The invitation to be profiled should be treated with some caution – profiles can be uncomplimentary 'hatchet jobs'.

Life in the Day

Feature which is a variant on the straightforward profile. Here, a famous person is profiled by concentrating on a typical day in their life.

My favourite books/year/influences

Features where individuals are invited to talk about subjects like the books they are taking on holiday, the time in their life they were most happiest, who the guiding influences in their lives are. By revealing this information, we learn a little more about them. Politicians asked these questions agonise for days over the answers - endeavouring to strike a balance between high-brow and low-brow, between culture and bloke-ishness. The ultimate torture is *Desert Island Discs*, a seemingly innocuous Radio 4 programme which can make or break reputations far more effectively than *Today*. The wrong choice of record - *Michael Bolton* or *Aqua* - can end a career faster than you can say cash for questions.

There's a story that does the rounds of a British Ambassador in the US being called up by a New York radio station to find out what he would like for Christmas - if he could have anything. Not wishing to distance himself from the average man in the street, he kept his wishes modest and replied that he'd like a pipe and new pair of slippers. Later that day he tuned into the station, with an audience in the hundreds of thousands, to hear his interview. *"The French Ambassador asked for world peace,"* related the interviewer, *"the Italian Ambassador said he'd like to see an end to hunger, and the British Ambassador asked for a pipe and a pair of slippers!"*

Dear Sir - Letters to the Editor

All publications have a letters page where readers are invited to share their thoughts on the world, comment on things they have read, or sometimes appeal for information. They range from the local paper's Letters Page, to the lofty heights of the *Times,* where sometimes letters from the famous and grand become news stories in themselves.

Some of the letters are from genuine members of the public, some from local dignitaries such as the Chairman of the local British Legion, or from national figures like charity chief executives. Some come from letter writing aficionados like the ubiquitous Keith Flett, Walter Cairns, Ian Flintoff, Gary Slapper, or Nicolas Walter of the 'Rationalist Press Association'.

Some are multi-signatory letters, almost a petition, designed to draw attention to some terrible injustice. A group of famous actors might put their name to a letter protesting against the closure of a local rep theatre, or left-leaning types like Tony Benn and Billy Bragg might co-sign a letter about the plight of the East Timorese. The *Guardian* on 9th December 1997 carried a letter protesting against lone parent benefit cuts with 26 signatories, including Glenys Kinnock MEP, the bosses of various charities such as the Childrens Society and Barnados, and academics like Ruth Lister and Jane Lewis. (Wags wondered what terrible falling-out must have occurred which meant that Melvyn Bragg hadn't signed it - his name is usually amongst the great and the good at the foot of these letters).

And some, letters page editors will tell you, come from the deranged and frightening casualties of modern society, written in green ink, with multiple underlinings, filled with bonkers stories about alien abductions and people following them.

Letters Page editors attempt a balance of 'real' people, the great and the good, and people writing on behalf of companies and campaigns. They will also balance the long and the short letters.

Because of the 'public access' ethos of letters pages, they are prime targets for the spin doctor. Here's how to do it.

Take aim...

If you write a letter to your local paper, it will almost certainly be published. Letters page editors are so desperate, that if the letter is in English, and is organised into sentences, it will be printed, even if it makes little sense.

THAT a collection of spoilt-brat, coke-snorting millionaire pop stars with the attention span of a goldfish have decided they've had enough of this Labour Government should cause no lost sleep (Blair dream disappears with a pop, March 11).

The Government wasn't elected to keep pop stars happy, but to make Britain better. With young people getting off the dole thanks to the windfall tax on utilities, with more money for schools and hospitals, the Government has done much to improve people's lives. The wunderkinds sell CDs whether there's a Tory or a Labour government. Unemployed teenagers get a real chance for work and training only when there's a Labour government.
Paul Richards.
London.

We do not publish letters where only an e-mail address is

A useful trick is to write a letter on a subject one week, and then have friends ready to write follow-up letters agreeing with you for the following week. You can even 'plant' letters disagreeing with yourself. There's nothing letters page editors like better than a heated debate.

In the nationals it's harder to get published, as there is greater competition. But even the *Times* has twenty letters to publish six days a week - so you're in with a chance.

In the United States, pressure groups, political parties, lobbyists, even companies, have developed networks of people who can be co-ordinated by the spin doctors to deluge newspapers with 'genuine' letters supporting a particular view. The same process is starting in this country. Local Tory associations have been doing it for decades. Lobbyists supporting the roads industry have been known to co-ordinate local residents and community action groups demanding that certain bypasses be built, and ensuring the message appears in the local papers.

Whenever a contentious issue such as abortion or fox-hunting hits the headlines, local papers are inundated with letters from both sides of the debate.

Leading up to the 1997 General Election the Labour Party organised a network of letter writers to pounce on anti-Labour columnists or opinions in national newspapers and magazines such as *New Statesman* and *Tribune*, with a remarkable degree of success. A telephone tree was established, and draft points to make were distributed by fax. Although the 'line' emanated from Tony Blair's office, enough chinese walls were erected to prevent the letter-writers being connected directly with the Labour high command. Over the months, letters appeared time after time, often from different people at the same address, supporting the Labour position.

...fire

A letter to a newspaper usually refers to an article in a recent edition. Usually the article will be a columnist's views, a 'think-piece' or a Leader, stating a strong view or position, and the letters referring to the article will take the contrary view. Some can be long, informed and expert views usually disagreeing with what a columnist has said; others can be short, even one line, with a sharp observation or pithy remark.

You must:

✔   Include your name, address and daytime telephone number,

✔   Have the words FOR PUBLICATION at the top,

✔   Address it to *Dear Sir*, or just *Sir*, (or *Dear Madam* or *Dear Editor* if you know or suspect the editor is female, such as Rosie Boycott at the *Independent*), and

✔   Begin by highlighting the issue to which you want to draw attention.

For example, this typical 'expert' letter in the *Times*: *'Sir, in an interesting article in your series on Victorian Britain ("Conquering disease as an enemy of Empire" August 15) Dr John Snow is referred to as Queen Victoria's obstetrician. In fact he was her anaesthetist; her obstetrician was Sir James Clark, etc.'* (*Times* 22nd August 1997).

This *Guardian* letter (13th December 1997) seeks to put the record straight: *'A Journalist of Peter Preston's standing really should know better than to cite that hoary old chestnut about the Inner London Education Authority's having banned competitive team games. This was one of the 'loony left' stories of the early 1980s, etc.'*

The letters in the *Manchester Evening News* are less prosaic. In local papers, writers, often without giving their names, can have their say: *'I was horrified to hear how many illegal immigrants are being smuggled into our country, which is already over-populated. Is it not time we copied the Americans and issued compulsory identity cards, with our photographs and thumb prints? Then dubious people would not be entitled to obtain money illegally. Dismayed Pensioner, Warrington.'* (8th December 1997)

Or this from the *Evening Standard:* *'At 16 I can buy tobacco and risk dying of cancer. At 18 I can buy alcohol and maybe get cirrhosis, but at 41 I can't buy a T-bone steak. There is something wrong.'* (9th December 1997)

For the spin doctor the point is not to show how clever you are by knowing the names of Queen Victoria's personal physicians, or that you've just heard the first cuckoo of the year, but to profile your organisation and get your message across. You should be reading the newspapers constantly on the look out for a 'letter' opportunity.

At the Royal National Institute for Deaf People (RNID), I earned brownie points by getting the Chief Executive into his favourite magazine, the *Economist,* with a letter about text telephones for deaf people. The opportunity was presented by an article about new technology in the office, and the letter to the *Economist* was along the lines of 'new IT will certainly help businesses communicate in the global marketplace - but there's another group who stand to benefit - deaf people'.

Once you've written your letter, it is usually best to fax it or email it to the number listed on the letters page itself. But if you're masquerading as a 'real person' posting it might add authenticity, as most people don't have instant access to faxes and email. It should be sent on the same day that the publication appears because, as discussed elsewhere SPEED KILLS.

Letter Writing Checklist

☑ Monitor the features and comment pages for possible openings to write a letter making your point or profiling your client

☑ Use the correct format: address, daytime number, "FOR PUBLICATION", reference to the article, and short, sharp sentences making a clear point.

☑ Send it quickly, preferably by fax or email marked *'For Letters Editor'*.

☑ Arrange for colleagues and friends to write letters responding to your letter - even disagreeing with you.

☑ Don't write too often to the same publication.

☑ Finally, expect to be edited.

Dear Diary

Diary columns are the light-hearted, amusing columns in newspapers or magazines, filled with gossip and anecdotes, appearing under a pseudonym such as 'Peterborough' (*the Daily Telegraph*) 'Ephraim Hardcastle' (*Daily Mail*) 'William Hickey' in the *Daily Express* 'Observer' in the *Financial Times* or 'Quidnunc' in the *Sunday Times*. The Diary in the *Times*, edited by Jaspar Gerard, is called simply *'The Times Diary'*

The name sometimes has a connection or meaning to the publication. The Daily Telegraph was printed in the Peterborough Building. The Times Diary was by-lined 'P.H.S.', and the paper was printed in Printing House Square. The Diarist in the political journal *Progress* is called 'Pilgrim'. In the *Evening Standard*, it's *'the Londoner'*. Often they take stories designed to plug a new film or book, to advertise an event or raise someone's profile. They can be used to trash someone's reputation, reveal a drunken celebrity's misdemeanours, float rumours too unsubstantiated for proper news pages, or even run vendettas.

If you believe, with Oscar Wilde, that the one thing worse than being talked about is not being talked about, or that even more misleading axiom that all PR is good PR, then Diaries are for you.

Each national paper's Diary is filled with stories of celebs, politicos, aristos and hacks. Here's a sample from the *Times* (13th December): *'Art Broken'* is a story about how a news camera crew visiting MP Alan Clark's home Saltwood managed to dislodge a Degas from the wall, and smashed the glass frame. We learn that William Hague's Christmas card carries a picture of William Pit the Younger. There's a story about opera singer Pavarotti being snubbed by the Barbados Opera Festival. The UBS/SBC Warburg merger means that John Major won't get to be chairman of the firm, we are informed. And finally there's a picture of new Bond Girl Cecile Thompson with Goldfinger Bond Girl Shirley Eaton. The stories represent a balanced collection of the light and trivial side of politics, the media, movies, opera and business.

The trick is to get to know a journalist on a Diary column personally, develop a bond of trust and establish yourself as a regular source of stories. This will help ensure that you don't end up as a Diary victim yourself, and if your name appears, it is because you want it too. Providing a flow of Diary stories can be a useful source of extra cash – most pay between £20 and £50 for a published story. Some establish accounts for 'regular contributors' (or 'snouts' depending on your perspective.)

But be warned - if your senior colleagues or famous friends begin to believe that any embarrassing information or private events like naked karaoke will be in the *Evening Standard* by 10am the next day, then you'll find yourself out of the loop pretty quickly.

And exercise caution: who lives by the Diary, can die by the Diary. Matthew Parris the Times columnist believes *'there's a special place in Hell'* reserved for Diary journalists, and they can indeed be evil creatures. If you use Diary columns too much, you may end up as the victim before long.

Mind Your Language

Written communication is essential to the spin doctor. The ability to write good, grammatical English which conveys the desired meaning to the right audience is one of the most important attributes of the skilled communicator. Call me old-fashioned, but I am one of those people who believe that school children should be taught how to read, write, and understand English.

The result of the fashionable teaching theories that allowed children to speak whatever dialect they chose, and ignore the 'bourgeois' rules of spelling and grammar, meant generations have grown up who wouldn't know an intransitive verb if it came up and pierced their nose.

The spin doctor understands, however that well-written, crisp, lively copy is the stuff of spin-doctoring. Whether you are producing a letter, briefing, memo, feature article, or news release, you must follow the rules.

The first set of rules concerns basic good grammar and spelling. Not that this book is a guide to good grammar – for that I especially recommend *'English for Journalists'* by Wynford Hicks (Routledge) or any of the texts listed in the bibliography. But if you seek to communicate you should take the time to learn when to write 'fewer' and when to write 'less', the difference between metaphor and similie, how to spell 'millennium' 'noticeable' and 'resuscitate', and when to use a semi-colon. And you should have noticed that I misspelled 'simile'.

The second set of rules concerns 'house style'. These are the self-imposed rules for writing which an organisation uses to cover all the grey areas not covered by formal grammar and spelling. House style rules should cover the use of accents on foreign words, Americanisms, capitals or lower case, captions, dates, numbers, foreign words, places, names, government and politics, hyphens, initials, italics, jargon, measures, and spelling.

These rules can differ from organisation to organisation. I worked in a press office where the use of capital letters was all but outlawed, even for titles like 'secretary of state'. The next place I worked insisted on capitals for titles, even 'Refuse Collector' (that's 'bin man' to you and me). So you have to learn the rules, then stick to them. If charged with establishing house style for your organisation, you can do worse than buying an established style guide, for example the FT Style Guide, and use that. There's no point in trying to re-invent the wheel.

Language must be tailored to the purpose in hand, and this is particularly true of dealing with the media. News releases must emulate, in style and content, the newspapers at which they are targeted. Feature articles must flow like the articles in that day's papers. They must appear to be crying out for inclusion. It must be easy for the journalist to turn your news release into copy which his subs will accept.

The best advice comes from one of this century's best writers, George Orwell: *"A scrupulous writer, in every sentence he writes, will ask himself at least four questions, thus: 'What am I trying to say? What words will express it? What image or idiom will make it clearer? Is this image fresh enough to have an effect?' And he will probably ask himself two more: 'Could I put it more simply? Have I said anything avoidably ugly?'"*

Keeping it simple and avoiding ugly words and phrases is the best test for all your writing. Writing short articles is harder than writing long ones.

You should avoid the worst excesses of 'tabloidese': the variant of English which exists only between the pages of the *Sun, Mirror* and *News of the World*. Tabloidese turns children to *'tots'*; reforms into *'shake-ups'*, dissenters into *'rebels'*, fires into *'infernos'*, disagreements into *'feuds'* or *'war'* and inquiries into *'probes'*. Viz comic parodied tabloidese with it spoof headline *'Gay Nazi Vicar in Killer Bees Storm'*, but most tabloids' headlines are almost self-parodies. Here are some recent ones: **OUTRAGE OF VICTIM IN 2-DAY QUIZ HELL** (*Sun*, 6th November) or **HERO PC IN KNIFE HORROR** (*Sun* 18th December) or **BENT COPS SCANDAL** (*Sun*, 19th December).

Your copy should be upbeat, 'newsy', crisp and concise, but avoid falling into tabloidese if possible.

Steer clear of clichés

You should avoid acid test, bitter end, burning issue, crying need, dead as a dodo, dark horse, horns of a dilemma, last but not least, sea of faces, take the bull by the horns, and this day and age.

If you can't give clichés a wide berth, steer clear of them, and avoid them like the plague, then rope in some other Joe to put pen to paper.

How about this string of clichés from David Mellor, writing in the *Evening Standard* sports pages about Alex Ferguson: *'Now he is the*

biter bit perhaps he'll change his tune, but I'm not holding my breath.'
Placing three clichés in one sentence is unforgivable.

Jargon and acronyms

Every organisation or profession uses its own jargon, short-hand and
acronyms. Jargon can be used by members of the same profession or
interest as a way of speeding communication, and a method of excluding outsiders from the group.

This is true of journalists, politicians, doctors, lawyers, and the
military, not to mention plumbers, darts-players, war-gamers and
taxi-drivers.

The corporate world is full of it: face time; run it up the flag-pole and
see who salutes it; I'll get my people to talk to your people; I've got a
window on the 26th; TQM; down-sizing and right-sizing; brainstorm-
ing session; singing from the same song sheet.

Because jargon by its nature is exclusionary, it must never find its way
into the communication between a spin doctor and his audiences.

I pity the US Army spin-doctor who had to explain this piece of nonsense uttered by General Schwartzkopf during the Gulf War: *'It is not
yet possible to get clear BDA in this area of the KTO. The continued
presence of Tripe A means a constant risk of allied personnel becoming KIA or WIA.'*

This is from a real news release: *'Repeated Methods Ltd today announced that it has grown exponentially in 1992, and that this acceler-
ating rate of adoption has firmly established their Fractal Transform
technology as a de-facto standard for still image compression'.* It is
the use of Latin which most amuses me in this prime example of a
news release destined for the bin.

This is from a letter I intercepted before it was sent from a local
council to residents: *'As part of a series of measures intended to help
revitalise your local town centre, the council will construct entry
treatments at the above locations.'* And what exactly do you think an

'entry treatment' is? It sounds vaguely medical, and certainly unpleasant. This letter, don't forget, was telling local people and businesses that roadworks were about to disrupt their lives, make them late for work, lose them customers, and generally make life miserable. The letter made things worse. Your communications should never be part of the problem you are trying to solve.

This same council laudably established a 'plain language initiative' to promote clear writing in council documents. The volunteers charged with implementing the scheme were dubbed 'PLAs' (plain language advisors). No one knew what a 'PLA' was, and so yet another piece of local government non-communication was created.

Get it Right

You should avoid obvious mistakes and misquotes in your copy (and in life generally), as these can detract from the seriousness of your message. I wrote a pamphlet on the Monarchy in 1996, filled with radical suggestions for reform including a new national anthem. Unfortunately I wrote (incorrectly) that the Welsh National Anthem was 'Men of Harlech'. At every meeting I have addressed on the subject since, someone, usually Welsh, has corrected the mistake. A mistake in a letter or news release might be turned against you by a hostile journalist or Diary columnist.

You should make a point of knowing all those smart-alec facts like: black and white are not colours; the Mother of Parliaments is England, not the House of Commons; it is the love of money that is at the root of all evil; the Republic of Ireland is part of the British Isles; Frankenstein refers to the creator, not the monster, and so on.

Every fact that you use must be correct. It's worth checking everything twice, because a factual error undermines your case and will haunt you for months, as Education Minister Stephen Byers found out when he gave the wrong answer to 7 times 8. And Dan Quayle will never forget when he told school children 'potato' has an 'e' at the end.

6 Spinning On The Air

"Despite the perfectly natural pants-wetting terror that appearing on radio and TV induces in most people, and the ever-present danger of making a fool of yourself in front of millions of strangers, there are tried and tested techniques which can help things go smoothly and provide reassurance."

Giving Interviews

Radio and TV news and current affairs programmes rely on people appearing and saying things. Sometimes they will be highly-paid reporters and presenters, sometimes 'vox pops' of people in the street, but often it will be people representing the view of an organisation or with something interesting to say, known as *'talking heads.'* That person could easily be you.

There are two reasons why you might be asked to do an interview: first, because you are the originator of news and the interview is about you, your organisation, your latest report, or whatever. Second, because the news story is about an issue in which you have a direct interest, and you are asked for comment, or expert opinion. The request from broadcast journalists (known as a 'bid') to appear usually comes with only a few hours notice. It often means being in a radio studio at some unearthly hour of the morning, or else in a TV studio late at night.

The programme will try to make the whole experience as easy as possible - they will arrange a car or taxi to take you to the studio and home afterwards, and offer you food and drink when you get there. Some programmes offer a small appearance fee which you can donate to charity, or keep.

Fielding the bid

When the bid comes in, you have to make a snap decision whether or not to take part. Will your appearance help or hinder your cause? Is it a set-up? You need to ascertain key information from the caller (usually a researcher or production assistant):

What is the programme? When does it go out? Why have they asked you? Who else is appearing? Has something happened to provoke the story (a new report you haven't read?) How long is the piece? Who is conducting the interview? What will the line of questioning be? All these need answers.

If the interview is just you and the interviewer it's is known as a 'one plus one'. If they interview and you and someone else at the same time, it's a 'one plus two'. The interview may be conducted remotely. On radio, the interview might be conducted over a landline phone, over an ISDN line, or from another studio. If the editor thinks you're worth it, you might end up in a 'radio car' - a kind of mobile studio which comes direct to you.

On television, they might conduct an interview live from another studio or from a location. If the interview is pre-recorded for television, a certain amount of trickery is involved. The crew will only have one camera, so they will film the interviewer asking the questions and nodding at your answers (a 'noddy') separately, and edit it in afterwards.

Perhaps the most important question you can ask is whether the interview is 'live' or pre-recorded? This information is the most important element of the interview, and changes your whole approach. A friend of mine was asked to do a local radio interview. He had been told (not by me) that if he made a mistake he should issue a string of swearwords, so that the broadcaster couldn't use the clip, and would have to ask the question again.

Having tripped over his words in one answer, he began to turn the air blue with filth that would make a docker blush. Only afterwards did he realise the interview was being broadcast live.

Most news stories on radio and TV are structured as a debate, because news stories usually contain an element of conflict. One person will make a claim, and an opponent will issue a counter claim. In a straightforward interview, usually with a politician, the interviewer will articulate the other side of the debate.

The process is best observed on the *Today* Programme, the most important news programme currently on air, but most news follows the same pattern: a new report from Friends of the Earth will claim that jet skis are dangerous and harmful to the environment. A spokesman from Friends of the Earth will come on the programme and say so, making the case using evidence in the report. Next, a spokesman from the Jet Ski Users Association will refute the evidence of the report, point to jet ski-ing's perfect safety record, and say the problem has been exaggerated. Your role is to fit into one side of this dialectic, and argue the toss with someone else.

The General News Service (GNS) is a good one to do if you are invited. GNS is the BBC service for all the local radio stations, and you sit in a studio in Broadcasting House and are interviewed by ten or twenty local radio stations in a row. It can take two or three hours, but one minute you're talking to people in Peterborough, then the next minute Slough, then Angelsey, Aberdeen, Bristol, etc.

Live interviews can be terrifying - even the most seasoned operators are tested by the likes of Jeremy Paxman or John Humphreys. I've been interviewed by both, and it's a scary experience. The advantage of being interviewed 'live' is that you are in control of the messages you give out. Your words cannot be edited, or juxtaposed with others, or taken out of context.

When the interview is pre-recorded you can take your time to prepare, and get it right. On pre-recorded radio, you will be asked to 'give some level', so the technicians can hear your voice and set their equipment. This is a good opportunity to get used to the microphone, and relax your voice. It's usually a good idea to drink some water just before speaking, because fear will work to dry your mouth.

Despite the perfectly natural pants-wetting terror that appearing on radio and TV induces in most people, and the ever-present danger of making a fool of yourself in front of millions of strangers, there are tried and tested techniques which can help things go smoothly and provide reassurance.

Appearance

In appearing on TV, appearance matters. Television is the most powerful medium, and people tend to remember what interviewees look like, not what they say. That means that smart unassuming business-like clothes and a clean, smart appearance are essential.

Kennedy is widely assumed to have beaten Nixon in the 1960 Presidential election TV debate, not because of policy differences, but because Nixon looked dishevelled, sweaty, unshaven and shifty, and Kennedy wore full make-up and looked smooth and trustworthy. Meanwhile the radio audience, who only *heard* the debate, overwhelmingly voted Nixon the winner.

If you are visiting someone's living room via the TV, the least you can do is look smart. Once I had to appear on *Newsnight* with half an hour's notice, after being tracked down by the BBC in a Indian restaurant in Soho. Without the time to change my clothes, the one feature of the interview that most people mentioned to me afterwards was not what I said, but the fact I was not wearing a shirt and tie. Many spokespeople who might expect bids from television at the last moment, keep an ironed white shirt and tie in their office just in case.

TV cameras have difficulty dealing with some bright colours such as scarlet. Bright blue should be avoided because it is used for Colour Separation Overlay, the process whereby images such as weather-maps are projected onto the screen. Small checks and 'dog-tooth' patterns can cause the messy appearance of 'strobing'. I appeared on *Tonight with Adam Boulton* on Sky TV on a panel with a chap whose tweed jacket strobed so badly he had to borrow a jacket from Adam Boulton.

Men should shave before going on TV. John Major, constantly in front of cameras, used to shave three times a day. It is normal for men appearing on TV to use make-up – usually some powder to take away shiny foreheads and five o-clock shadow, and to disguise bags under the eyes. In studio interviews, the interviewer is taken to make-up beforehand. In interviews outside or at your own location, the TV crew will usually not have any make-up. Most spin doctors have a small make-up compact in their desks, just in case. That's my excuse and I'm sticking to it.

A useful tip for the chaps is to remember to take it off. Straight after the aforementioned appearance on *Wogan*, I had to get on a train for a meeting in Manchester. Only when the train pulled into Manchester Piccadilly some three hours later did I realise that I was still wearing full TV face make-up, which explained some of the funny looks from passengers.

If seated for a TV interview, sit on the back of your jacket to stop it riding up and making you look hunch-backed. Straighten your tie. Avoid distracting jewellery, flashy ties or waistcoats. If you want what you have to say to be taken seriously, look sober and respectable, and if you want people to listen to your message, then avoid distractions like wild hand-gestures and violent nods of the head.

Women should check their blouse buttons are done up (a visible cleavage can distract from your message), make sure their earrings match and check for lipstick on teeth.

Body language

Your posture and body language are as important as what you say. You must try (and it is very hard) to control your non-verbal communication. Keep your feet still and avoid the 'foot-flap' - the non-verbal signal for '*I want to get out of here.*' Don't shuffle about in your seat, because that makes you look uncomfortable and shifty. Don't close your eyes for longer than a blink, or touch your nose, when answering, because that implies you are lying or have something to cover up. Sit up straight, smile, maintain eye contact, and keep your hands and feet still.

Preparation

Preparation is the key to a successful interview. You must think it through in advance, and practice what you want to say. On radio, you can have your notes in front of you as you speak (but be careful not to rustle them). You should also identify weak spots in your argument, and be prepared to answer hostile questions. Write down your key points and rehearse them out loud. The sound of an answer is very different from how it appears on paper. While fielding the bid, or even as you wait to go on air, you ask what the first question will be (the interviewer might even tell you.)

Ignore the Question

The most important technique in dealing with media interviews is to completely ignore the question. You should decide what you want to say, and say it. The interviewer's question is merely your cue to say your piece.

This technique is nothing new. One of the first British politicians to properly understand the workings of TV was Labour leader Harold Wilson. According to Gerald Kaufman, his then spin-doctor, Wilson *'didn't go to the TV studio to answer the questions. The questions were an irrelevance which had to be listed to...he decided what he wanted to say – the message he wanted to communicate to the people who were watching and then, regardless of the questions that were put to him, he said what he meant to say.'* Harold Wilson won four General Elections.

Similarly, Liberal Democrat Peer, David Steel, admits: *'I always make a habit of writing down three or four points I want to make and proceed to make them regardless of the questions the erudite interrogators or their even more erudite researchers have made up.'*

And in the interests of political balance here's former Tory Prime Minister Edward Heath: *'The thing to do before a big programme is to be clear in your mind about what you want to say, because the interviewer will always try and deal with something else.'*

Constructing your sound-bite

When you have decided what you want to say, you need to condense your thoughts into short, sharp digestible chunks, widely known as 'sound-bites'.

'Sound-bite' is a term born in the USA, and stems particularly from the 1988 Presidential election between George Bush and Michael Dukakis. It means the short, snappy and memorable phrase used for radio and TV. The pressures of the media mean that no-one gets more twenty or thirty seconds to speak in a news broadcast.

Soundbites are shrinking: it has been estimated that the length has dropped from 40 seconds in the late 60's to 20-30 seconds by the 80's. By the 1992 General Election party leaders could expect 22 seconds on the BBC's *Nine O'Clock News*, and just 16 seconds on ITN's *News at Ten.*

Soundbites have been denounced as undermining and trivialising the political process, by not allowing arguments to be expanded and explained. I disagree. I believe that it is no bad thing if politicians are disciplined into encapsulating their message into understandable, coherent phrases - that helps the democratic process. Margaret Thatcher says in her *Downing Street Years* that before winning the 1979 election the Tories had *'taken apprenticeships in advertising and learnt how to put a complex and sophisticated case in direct, clear and simple language.'*

When a politician fails to properly convey his or her meaning, as Gordon Brown uncharacteristically managed with his phrase *'post-neo classical endogenous growth theory'*, they are rightly lampooned. And the sound-bite is really only a new version of the slogan - which has been in politics for centuries. Instead of distributing his lengthy political tomes to the Russian masses, Lenin invented a soundbite to encapsulate what the Bolsheviks stood for: 'Bread, Peace and Land'.

During the 1964 General Election campaign Harold Wilson used to judge the moment in his speeches when the BBC would start to broadcast it live, and switch his remarks to soundbite-based messages which he wanted the viewers to hear, not his party faithful audience.

Your sound-bites needn't be candidates for inclusion in the Oxford Dictionary of Quotations, but should express your point in a lively and hard-hitting way.

Recent examples of well-received sound-bites include Tony Blair's *'Tough on crime, tough on the causes of crime.'* and William Hague's *'A fresh start'.*

The current Government creates soundbites by placing '*The Peoples*' in front of things (The Peoples Princess, The Peoples Lottery, The Peoples Government).

Margaret Thatcher had a good line in soundbites: '*The lady's not for turning*', '*There is no alternative*', and '*Enemy within.*'

Franklin D Roosevelt had the '*New Deal*' and '*The only thing we have to fear is fear itself*'.

Winston Churchill used: '*Blood, sweat and tears*', '*This was their finest hour*' and '*Iron curtain*'. My favourite is JF Kennedy who gave us: '*The New Frontier*', *Let us never negotiate out of fear. But let us never fear to negotiate*', '*Ask not what your country can do for you, ask what you can do for your country*', and '*Mankind must put an end to war or war will put an end to mankind*'. JFK was fond of his inversions.

Try and be figurative, without being clichéd. Use visual imagery, if possible, and make statistics come alive with real examples that people can relate to. Margaret Thatcher used to explain complex economic issues by talking like a housewife. Be clear what you want to say, and say it. And then keep repeating it like a mantra until the interview is over.

Avoiding the chop

Ruth Turner, a campaigner against homelessness in Manchester, regularly appears on radio and television in support of her cause. She has a valuable trick that she often uses in pre-recorded radio interviews. We shall christen it the Turner Breathing Technique, and I shall let Ruth explain it in her own words: '*If you make your point in two sentences, the pressure of time often means that the second sentence will be edited out, losing the force of your argument. You should therefore say the same words, but breathe halfway through the second sentence, so that there are no natural pauses for the editor to cut.*'

It works like this: '*There are over a thousand people under the age of 20 living on the streets. (pause for breath) The Government must act quickly before winter sets in.*' Here the second sentence is destined for the chop.

'There are over a thousand people under the age of 20 living on the streets and the Government (pause for breath) must act quickly before winter sets in.' In this example, the clip is harder to edit, and you might get longer exposure as a result.

In other words, you make it extremely hard to slice the clip in two, so the editing gets done to someone else.

Beware the pitfalls

Appearing on radio or TV, even a local station, will have a huge impact. If you do it, you will be surprised how many people comment on your appearance afterwards. You should be keen therefore to avoid the pitfalls.

There are the terrible mistakes of the rich and famous to serve as reminders of our own failings. Who can forget George Best appearing drunk as a Lord on *Wogan*? The lesson here is to not get drunk beforehand (which means avoiding all the free booze in the hospitality suite before going on air).

Never lose your temper (although a good interviewer might try to make you lose your rag; it makes great TV). You should be polite, but firm, and try to get the last word. You should try to use the interviewer's name, but only once (any more and it becomes a distraction or sounds obsequious).

Stay on your guard. John Major's Government was dominated by reports of what his Euro-sceptic 'Bastards' were up to. The name Bastards came from an unguarded remark Major made to Michael Brunson in 1993 in-between TV interviews, while cameras were still transmitting to other broadcasters. Labour's broadcasting officer in the early eighties, Mish Tullar, got one over Michael Heseltine in January 1993, when the Deputy Prime Minister was preparing for a live interview at the BBC studios at 4 Millbank. He was told the interview would focus on the interest rate cut which had happened that morning. Heseltine admitted he knew nothing of the cut. Mish Tullar, in another part of the Millbank complex, saw Heseltine on an internal TV monitor and listened into the sound feed which was picking up every word he said.

Within minutes, Tullar was on the phone to political reporters with the news that Heseltine didn't know what was going on. Since that incident, the BBC at Millbank has introduced a security swipe card system to stop spin doctors hanging around picking up information.

President Ronald Reagan went one better: when asked to speak to provide a sound level check for a radio interview he announced the USA would start bombing Russia in five minutes time.

So – be careful what you say at any point before and after the interview – you never know who may be listening.

Following up

Try and video or audio record your appearance, and watch it afterwards with a critical eye. Watch out for foot-flapping or eye-scratching, use of the *'crutch phrases'* we all use to prop us up such as *'you know'*, *'and so on'*, and *'I have to say that...'* You can learn from your mistakes, and be better next time.

Remember, too, that if you feel you've been stitched up you have the right to complain (See Making Complaints).

TV and Radio - Dos and Don'ts

Do

✔   Plan what you want to say in advance and rehearse
✔   Think in short "sound bites"
✔   Stay calm, relaxed, and comfortable
✔   Ignore the question - say what you want to say, regardless of the interviewer.
✔   Use the interviewers name - but only once
✔   Wear smart clothes on TV (keep spare clothes reserve)
✔   Sit on the back of your jacket to stop it riding up
✔   Wear make-up (especially for men)
✔   If possible, men should shave just before appearing

Don't

✗   Relax your guard even when the interview is over - sound is still being picked up.

✗   Look directly at the camera

✗   Accept offers of free alcoholic drinks

✗   Try to be funny

✗   Use jargon or technical language

✗   Wear distracting clothes or accessories

✗   Rustle papers or clank jewellery on the radio

✗   Swear, smoke, chew gum

✗   Walk out before the end of the interview, or after the interview while the cameras are still on.

On Line One...

Radio and TV Phone Ins

The broadcast equivalent to *Letters to the Editor* is the radio phone-in, which also appears on certain television programmes such as *Election Call* or *Conference Call*. This can be an excellent way of both making your point, and putting the programme guest on the spot, or supporting them, depending on your viewpoint. Politicians hate phone-ins because they are unpredictable, and members of the public do not play by the rules of interviewing which presenters usually abide by. A politician who has mastered Jeremy Paxman, Peter Sissons or Kirsty Wark can easily be kebabbed by an ordinary member of the public. Politicians cannot be rude and dismissive to members of the public in the same way they can to interviewers.

Margaret Thatcher was famously and uncharacteristically caught off-guard during the 1983 General Election when she appeared on a phone-in on BBC TV's *Nationwide*. A member of the public, Mrs Diana Gould, directly challenged Mrs Thatcher over the sinking of the Argentine cruiser the Belgrano during the previous year's Falklands War. Thatcher was caught out, pressed again and again by Mrs Gould, and came from the encounter visibly riled. That was the only occasion during the 1983 general election when anyone managed to get the better of her.

US President George Bush was a victim of a superb piece of spin doctoring in the 1992 Presidential elections when he appeared on *Larry King Live*. As Bush appeared to have side-stepped Larry King's and callers questions on his involvement in the Iran-Contra scandal, a call came in from a 'Mr Stephanopoulos calling from Little Rock, Arkansas'. The call, from Bill Clinton's communications chief, appeared as though he had phoned the public access phone numbers and got lucky. Stephanopoulos, armed with proof of Bush's involvement in arms for hostages deals, embarrassed and humiliated the President live on national TV. In reality, the call had been negotiated between the Clinton war room and the *Larry King Live* producer Tammy Haddad, and the stunt hit the front pages the next day.

Phone-in checklist

- ☑ Monitor the phone-in programmes on radio and TV, and spot opportunities to get your point across
- ☑ Phone in plenty of time – you may have to hang on for a while
- ☑ Make your point immediately and forcefully, without being aggressive or rude
- ☑ Have a follow-up question ready (preferably a googlie to throw the interviewee or politician)
- ☑ If you get through to a national politician on a phone-in as part of a local campaign, take notes of the answer and spin the story to the local papers or relevant trade mag.

Other Ways Of Spinning

*"An empty press conference is the stuff
of spin doctors' nightmares."*

The News Conference

The best advice I can give on whether to hold a news conference is *don't*. They're usually more trouble than they're worth. The first question to ask yourself should be: is the story important enough to warrant a press conference? If the story is major - a new premier league football signing, a resignation from the Cabinet, the Spice Girls splitting up, then the amount of media interest will warrant a news conference. If you are announcing the winner of the local darts league or a change of venue for the Retired Men's Club monthly meeting, forget it.

Are you absolutely sure?

An empty press conference is the stuff of spin doctors' nightmares. In the early 1990s one bright young press officer found himself charged with organising a news conference in the Jubilee Room of the House of Commons jointly for a leading Labour politician and an animal welfare group. The subject was the threat posed to the rare loggerhead turtle by tourists on the Greek Islands (the noise of late night Ouzo drinking and night flights was stopping the turtles - but not the tourists - from breeding). Despite meticulous planning and phone-rounds, not one single journalist turned up. Not one. It was highly embarrassing for all concerned, and the press officer in question got a rollicking - I should know, dear reader, for that press officer was me.

So - always judge whether a news event warrants a formal style news conference, and even if your clients or employers demand to have their egos flattered, counsel against any over-estimation of the news value of the story.

If you do want to hold such as event, as with all media relations, it must be planned.

Choose your venue

Choose your venue wisely. To entice journalists away from their desks, it must be convenient for them. A story about rural poverty amongst crofters in the Highlands will not receive much coverage if the news conference in held in a rural crofters cottage up a mountain. A group of crofters staging a press conference in central Edinburgh or London have a much better chance. The mountain has to come to Mohammed.

So pick a central location near the news centre in your town and region. Choose a room large enough to accommodate the expected number of journalists, but not so large that it looks empty even with twenty hacks. If you expect television crews, ensure that there is space near the front for them to set up their equipment, and a power supply nearby. Make sure there is a backdrop with your organisational logo and name. The top table should be covered, and uncluttered by cups of coffee and newspapers. It is usually the spin doctors job to ensure that all the bases are covered, so that bringing an emergency kit of bluetack, scissors, marker pens, etc., is essential.

Who speaks?

The line-up for press conferences can be a matter of great controversy, as everyone wants the limelight. But the spin doctor must be disciplined and keep the top table from looking like a police identity parade.

The best approach is a chairman to introduce the speakers, the lead spokesman for the organisation (the Chairman, Chief Executive, etc.) to provide the corporate line and an expert (Head of Research, the author of the report being launched, etc.) to provide factual expert information as a backup. If the story is a new factory opening in Salford or about aid for Albania, then invite some Salfordians/Albanians (don't get them mixed up) to sit in the audience. Remember to tell your story through people. A new factory is not a building, it is, "jobs, regeneration, hope". Journalists will want to speak to the people that your new venture will benefit, so make sure they've all been briefed and learnt their lines.

Allow plenty of time

For journalists to actually turn up, you must lay the ground well in advance. A 'calling notice' must be issued, and Forward Planning and News Diary sections of news organisations must be alerted. Invite specific journalists, and give them a call to find out if they have received the information. Do NOT badger journalists for an answer to your invitation - it isn't a dinner party. Journalists, especially in the broadcast media, operate on an hour-by-hour basis and their appearance at your event will depend on that day's news. So luck plays a part.

Get the timing right

Timing is important: mid morning is best because journalists on dailies are hours away from deadlines, and the lunch time bulletin broadcasters have time to edit the footage. But even mid-morning is too late for evening papers like the London Evening Standard, so you'll have to brief them in advance, under a strict embargo.

Decide the line – and keep it short

When briefing the top table, you must ensure that they are clear about what is to be said, which of them will say it, and for how long. There must be no duplication, nor a cigarette-paper's width of difference between what is being said by the spokespeople, or in the written material you have issued. Presentations or remarks must be short - less than five minutes.

The meat of the news conference for journalists is the 'Q and A's' (Questions and Answers). This is the journalist's chance to follow up their own angle on the story. Q and A's must be rehearsed in advance, and the spin doctor must second guess every possible journalists' question and prepare an answer for the spokespeople on the top table.

Keep the hacks happy

If you have a budget for such things, you should provide journalists with refreshments, copies of the remarks and background notes, and perhaps even freebie give-aways such as pens or mousemats.

There should be a list of journalists expected to turn up, and perhaps name badges. One trick is to recast your news conference as a 'lecture' or 'launch' and invite interested parties from partner organisations, academics, anyone really, to make the room look full and make the event seem significant.

Is the medium the message?

Sometimes *where* is more important than *what* is being said. A good choice of venue can add to the message you wish to get across. A news conference launching a new software product should be launched in a hi-tech building, not a dusty old museum.

When Tony Blair was running for Leader of the Labour Party against John Prescott and Margaret Beckett in 1994 he launched his campaign at his local constituency Labour Club in Trimden Colliery, County Durham. He surrounded himself with enthusiastic supporters from the local working-class community. Before he had said a word, Blair had differentiated himself from his opponents who both held Westminster press conferences flanked by other MPs, and established his image as a man of the people.

Whilst there are plenty of venues - hotels, town halls, conference centres - in most towns which can be hired for a news event, why not consider an unusual venue or one which illustrates your story. A local church group launching a week of inter-faith understanding might hold their event at the local synagogue or temple. The message would be in journalists' minds before a word had been spoken.

The flipside is that a misjudged choice of venue can be a PR disaster: the Trades Unions Congress holding its press launch at the Natural History Museum, for example. (A version of this actually happened to Bill Morris, the transport union boss, who found himself speaking at a meeting with an enormous painting of a carthorse behind him. The carthorse is the image used by trade unions' enemies to portray them as lumbering and old-fashioned.) Always check what's going on behind you.

Following Up

At the end of the formal part of the news conference (which should last no more than 30-45 minutes, offer individual interview to the broadcasters, and provide a separate quiet room for radio interviews.

After the event, follow it up by writing to the journalists who came, thanking them and offering more information and interviews. Especially important is to ring round those journalists who didn't come, and brief them, if they want it, on what was said.

News Conferences Checklist:

☑ Do you really need to hold a news conference? Will a couple of phone-calls do the job as easily? Always err on the side of caution.

☑ Choose a venue that people can get to easily, with a backdrop, and covered top-table

☑ Allow no more than three people to do the talking

☑ Target the right journalists and get the event into news organisation's forward planning systems

☑ Prepare and co-ordinate the statements in advance, and rehearse Q and A's.

☑ The formal part should only last 45 minutes at most.

☑ Have plenty of supporting information available, and offer interviews

☑ Follow up the event for those who came, and those who didn't.

Stunts

It might be that the way to get attention and get your message across is to organise a stunt. Stunts are events which appeal to the journalists sense of the unusual or unique. They intrigue and excite the person seeing the stunt in the media. Stunts usually have a purpose - to sell products or to make a point. Sometimes they're designed simply to make some sad individual famous for fifteen minutes. Having an all-over body tattoo or eating an entire London Routemaster Bus fall into this category.

The Beatles staged a concert on the roof of the Apple Building in central London in 1969, causing traffic chaos and plenty of publicity. The stunt was later copied by the rock band U2.

In 1997 a character known as Swampy became temporarily famous. Swampy and his chums were anti-roads protesters, who would go to extra-ordinarily dangerous lengths to delay roads building programmes by digging tunnels and concreting themselves into the path of bulldozers. Swampy pulled one of the best stunts of the year by announcing that he would be standing as a candidate in the General Election. He faxed his hand-scrawled announcement to the newsrooms, and the story hit the headlines. Only afterwards did Swampy reveal that it was a hoax. Perhaps journalists should have spotted two give-aways (a) Swampy is an anarchist and rejects parliamentary democracy, and (b) the announcement came on April 1st.

Cedric the Pig became famous in 1995 as the row over privatised utilities' executive pay reached its height. Phil Woolas, spin doctor for the GMB trade union, introduced Cedric, (named after Cedric Brown, chairman of British Gas) to the media – and they loved him. Cedric became the symbol of the 'snouts in the trough' beneficiaries of the Tories' sell-off of state-owned utilities, and appeared all over the television, radio and press. Cedric's retirement even merited a news item on *London Tonight*.

John Prescott donned a wetsuit and aqualung and swam down the Thames to make a point about pollution. The campaigning group Surfers Against Sewage went one further – they used a gigantic 'inflatable poo' to float in the sea at pollution blackspots to illustrate their point.

Many groups organise stunts outside Downing Street to protest about some burning issue. I once got on television with some Student friends by pulling an admittedly rather-lame stunt involving sleeping bags outside Downing Street in protest against Mrs Thatcher's housing policy. The most recent proponents of the Downing Street stunt were a group of extremist, disabled rights campaigners who splattered the pavement with red paint to protest against the Labour Government. Not very original, but it scored with all the television news programmes.

The gay rights group Outrage depends upon daring and attention-grabbing stunts to make their points. Their stunts have included a mass gay 'kiss-in' in Trafalgar Square, and the laying of a wreath to commemorate gay victims of war at the Cenotaph. These stunts cause offence to some, and therefore create a rumpus in the media, which is exactly what Outrage want.

Toy company Mattel, as part of their promotion of the Barbie Doll, arranged for an entire street in Salford, near Manchester, to be painted bright pink. The company promised the residents of Ash Street to give their homes a new coat of paint after a month, and they donated money to community projects. The stunt appeared in the nationals, and on ITN News At Ten.

Stunts are for those who don't care too much about the seriousness with which they are treated, or by those - such as campaigning groups - who feel the media will not take any notice if they play by the rules. Use stunts with care - but recognise they can play an important role in grabbing the media's attention and gaining coverage.

Stunts checklist

- ☑ Make sure what you are doing is legal, and will not get you arrested (unless being arrested is part of your stunt).
- ☑ Assemble the main players, and costumes, props, well in advance.
- ☑ Do a recce of the location in advance – make sure it is still accessible (time in recce is seldom wasted, as the army says)
- ☑ Alert the media – send out advance notice to picture-desks and television stations
- ☑ Have your own 'in-house' photographer on hand to record the event for your own purposes.

Photo-Opportunities

A picture is worth a thousand words, and part of your spin doctoring may involve using photo-opportunities.

Photo-opportunities (or photo-opps) are events staged purely for the benefit of the news cameras, or for photos in-house to be taken and sent out yourself, and used to illustrate a message in a stark visual fashion. Martin Rosenbaum *in 'From Soapbox to Soundbite'* says, *'photo opportunities work by fostering impressions. They do not assert clear propositions which can be the focus of argument, they establish connotations and communicate subliminally.'*

For example, during the 1997 General Election, Tony Blair made a visit to Dover - a key seat for Labour to win. But the photo-opp for the visit, of Blair standing alone against a backdrop of the White Cliffs, had a message far beyond the voters of Dover. The image of a man standing alone against the great symbol of Britain's freedom and independence communicated Labour's messages about Blair being a future great leader, the party's patriotism, and the party's willingness to 'stand up to Europe.'

During the 1983 General Election Margaret Thatcher was photographed in front of the largest union jack in the world - on the hanger door of the factory she was visiting. The image - of *'Last Night of the Proms'* patriotism - reminded the voters of her victory in the Falklands War the previous year, without a word being said. Indeed if Thatcher had tried to overtly use the Falklands War during the campaign, she might have been accused of exploiting the situation.

These can become hackneyed. Lottery winners are usually shown with a huge bottles of champagne and beautiful women to show their success. Donors to charity set up photo-opps with oversized cardboard cheques. New buildings are launched by some business executive with a hard-hat and trowel laying a brick. Politicians love being photographed with nurses, or babies, or in computer factories.

Business spin doctors run into the problem of making their bosses - grey suited captains of industry and commerce - look interesting and dynamic. The solution is usually to create photo-opps of these boring-looking men engaged in interesting activities: so, for example, brewery bosses will appear drinking beer. A recent photo-opp set up to illustrate the deal between American Airlines and British Airways placed BA boss Bob Ayling and American Airlines boss Don Carty alongside each other draped in their respective national flags, and carrying model aeroplanes. The result: two embarrassed-looking executives looking faintly foolish.

Some can be more imaginative. Virgin boss Richard Branson and radio DJ Chris Evans staged a photo-opp to launch their new partnership at Virgin Radio - they invited the snappers in to photograph them both naked from the waist up lying together in bed. The picture was intriguing and memorable, and illustrated the story - that these two big players were 'getting into bed'.

One master of the photo-opp is Phil Woolas MP, former spin-doctor for the GMB trade union. He organised a series of famous photo-opps for his union, including persuading union boss John Edmonds to be photographed placing his union's block vote in a huge shiny rubbish bin to exemplify the end of the block vote at Labour Party conference. Woolas is also the man who put 'GMB' on the shirt of every player of Fulham football club by being the first trade union to sponsor a football club.

Woolas's love of the well-taken photo that tells a tale was taken a little far in May 1997. As a new MP, Woolas abused his position and took a snap of Brian Mawhinney eating alone on the House of Commons terrace. The photo duly appeared in the *Daily Mirror*, along with a story crowing about the Tories' defeat. Woolas had to apologise to the House.

During the 1997 General Election the local Labour Party in Coventry got their photo-opp in the nationals: they lined up 22 activists in identical comedy John Major masks (one for each tax rise under the Tories, they explained). Labour candidates were sent weekly memos with ideas for photo-opportunities, and some worked quite well. One involved a hamper of shopping costing exactly the amount that the Tories had taken extra in tax.

Four Conservative candidates in the same election came up with a good local photo-opportunity. They set up a photo-opp with a local newsagent to protest at the amount of red tape hampering the newsagent's business: it involved tying the poor chap up with actual red tape. The snappers loved it. As well as the locals, the trades picked it up and the story appeared in *Retail News Agent* and *CTN News*.

They can backfire - Clare Short's photo-opp involving her with landmine clearing equipment and a 'Danger Mines' sign caused an outcry as she was accused of copying Diana, Princess of Wales. In the early eighties Margaret Thatcher allowed herself to be photographed alone in an industrial wasteland - the story was supposed to be about industrial regeneration. Instead the photo was used to attack the Tories' record of factory closures and business failures. John Gummer was roundly condemned for force-feeding his daughter a beefburger as a photo-opportunity to prove British beef is safe.

You should always be aware of potential embarrassments in the background such as shop names like *Loser and Loser*, or parts of your slogan on the backdrop which can be cropped to make new words. Politicians employ 'advance teams' to recce places they intend to visit, and avoid embarrassments. During a visit to a war museum, Tony Blair had to be bundled away from cameramen by special branch officers when they realised he was about to be photographed in front of a swastika.

Journalists are told about photo-opportunities via a type of news release called a 'Notice of Photo-opportunity'. The basic format is similar to a standard news release, but it is targeted at the photo-desk, not the news desk, and the information contained is the exact time, place, and purpose of the photo-opp. Photos can be distributed in digital format to newsrooms by the Press Association.

Photo-opps checklist

☑ Set up your location - and check for embarrassments in the background

☑ Have an indoor fall-back if your location is outdoors and it rains

☑ Issue a 'notice of photo-opportunity' news release to picture desks

Using a Photographer

If you want total control over the photograph, you can commission your own photographs and distribute them to your chosen newspapers, with news releases. This is not a cheap option, but if you have the budget it can be effective.

The same rules apply as for setting up a photo-opp: make sure your photograph is fresh, eye-catching and expresses the point of the story. Avoid men in suits shaking hands, groups of people giving the thumbs-up, or over-sized novelty cheques. Try unusual angles, interesting locations, and attention-grabbing set-ups. The human brain, whether male or female, is attracted to beautiful faces (which is why women's magazines have beautiful women on the cover), so use attractive people where possible, without being too obvious or sexist. Use the photographer as a consultant, not merely a technician, because they will have more experience of what makes a good picture and what doesn't.

You should choose your photographer with care. The NUJ *Freelance Directory*, *Hollis Annual* and local *Yellow Pages* list photographers for hire. Note, however, that the word '*photographer*' covers a multitude of sins, from local wedding and portrait specialists, to famous and rich fashion photographers. You should ascertain whether the photographer specialises in what you want, and always get a price first, including hidden extras like contact sheets, travel expenses, printing and copying. You need to decide whether to commission black and white or colour. This decision is made on the basis of your target media - if you're targeting a glossy magazine, use colour. If is it the local paper, use black and white.

When distributing your photographs, avoid the scatter-gun approach, and try to sell-in the photo to the picture editor over the phone. Offer to bike or hand-deliver the photos over for the picture editor to have a look at, rather than describing them over the phone. The less money a publication has, the more likely it is to welcome a photograph. Local papers and trades and technicals cannot afford to have snappers covering every event and so are more likely to use a photograph you sent them. Many trade and technical titles carry a section on the people moving jobs or winning awards or contracts in the particular sector or industry, and always welcome simple headshots of the people concerned.

If you have written an article for a publication, offer pictures to illustrate it, and a mugshot of the author to go alongside the by-line.

Distribute photos using hard-backed envelopes, and always caption and brand the photograph, saying who, where, and what it is, when it was taken, and the contact name, address and number for its return or further information.

In-house press offices will build up a stock of press photographs of their organisation's leading lights (which, if kept on file for a number of years, can be used to embarrass them at retirement parties), and 'stock shots' of their products or photographs which illustrate their cause or concern. At the Royal National Institute for Deaf People, we were forever being badgered for pictures of people using sign language or wearing hearing aids.

Using a photographer checklist

- ☑ Can you afford it?
- ☑ Choose the right photographer, with the right specialism
- ☑ Decide what you want - locations or studio, number of prints, colour or black and white?
- ☑ Target your media, don't mail out at random
- ☑ Talk to the picture editor, not just the newsdesk
- ☑ Don't reinvent the wheel each time - build up a photo-library of stock shots and mugshots

Spinning On The Net

The Internet is the single most important development for news and media organisations since the invention of television. Take-up rates are expanding exponentially. According to recent research, online domestic services will jump nine-fold over the next five years, fuelling a massive growth in opportunities for spin doctoring, and not just to nerds in anoraks.

Most organisations now have websites, and news is increasingly available on-line. No spin doctor, even the most techno-phobic, can afford to ignore the awesome potential of the net.

The Internet will have a major influence on public opinion over the next decade. Rogue sites and hostile sites can quickly, cheaply and very effectively generate negative (often untrue) publicity, while acting as a focal point for campaigns and action targeted against the organisation. At the same time, rumours, (both true and false) can be given fresh life through newsgroups, notice boards and chat rooms.

The spin doctor of the future will attempt to influence these newsgroups and chatrooms just as 'phone-ins and letters pages are targets today.

Net Spinning Checklist

☑ Do not underestimate the power and importance of the Net. Just because you don't know how to use it, it doesn't mean millions of others don't.

☑ Monitor newsgroups, chat rooms, rogue sites and your competitors' activity on the net.

☑ Intervene if possible, and get your messages across, but only after a monitoring or you may get 'flamed'.

☑ Build the Internet into your spin doctoring plans wherever possible.

8 Advanced Spinning

"If things go wrong, there is usually a way of turning the story to your advantage. Don't panic, but instead think how your actions in a crisis might leave a positive lasting image."

Dealing With a Crisis

E ven for the best spin doctor, things can go wrong. Companies can be hit by unexpected disasters such as terrorist action, contamination of their product, or challenges to their safety record. Governments can be rocked by sexual or financial scandals. People within businesses can find themselves on the wrong end of rumours and gossip. Your family members' actions may drag you into the limelight.

Crisis management is a key skill for the spin doctor. The best time to plan for a crisis is when there isn't one, and many large companies keep a 'crisis manual' on the shelf with a set of procedures, and regularly practice them.

What's happening?

First of all you need all the facts. The crisis team needs to be at the centre of the information flow. All channels of information should be open, and the full picture needs to be established quickly. The first few hours are essential – if you have to wake Chief Executives up in the small hours, then do it. The story will develop one of two ways: either the way the organisation at the centre of the crisis is dealing with it, or way of the people effected by the crisis complaining that the organisation responsible is not doing enough. The way airlines deal with passenger delays provides good examples of both good and bad crisis management. Some get it right; some horribly wrong.

Focus the source of information

The worst thing in a crisis is to have journalists getting informa-tion from unauthorised sources. If members of staff, eye-witnesses, and various spokesmen are giving different stories, the result will be conflicting information, and you will lose control of the story. In a crisis, there should be a single, authoritative and informed source for journalists.

Be honest

Honesty is usually the best policy. If you are at fault, then admit it, and explain what you are doing to put it right. If attempts are made at a cover-up and you are found out, the damage will be much more severe. Journalists will respect and trust the spin doctor who doesn't try to stonewall and gloss over obvious faults.

Take responsibility

The issue of Formula One boss Bernie Eccleston's donation of £1 million to the Labour Party (and the Labour Government subse-quently exempting Formula One from the tobacco advertising ban) is a good example of how a crisis can come from nowhere. The issue became a major news story for days, and marked, for many, the end of Labour's honeymoon after the election. The major part of the problem seemed to be that no one had spotted the danger of adverse publicity from Mr Eccleston's donation and the subsequent decision on tobacco sponsorship, and the story ran out of control. No one seemed to know what was going on. In the end, the Prime Minister appeared in his first full-length television interview to apologise for the affair, and to take personal responsibility (even though he knew nothing about it.)

Do Something

If something goes wrong, the media will want to know what you are going to do about it, not least to have a further aspect of the story to cover. Being sorry isn't enough. You need to be seen taking action. This might include a full inquiry; compensation for victims; sacking someone; changing procedures so that it can never happen again. When an alleged scandal involving John Prescott's son and the sale of some council houses in Hull broke in March 1998, a Government investigative team was dispatched immediately, and found no evidence of wrongdoing, thus killing the story dead. The story must be moved on.

Turn the story to your advantage

If things go wrong, there is usually a way of turning the story to your advantage. Don't panic, but instead think how your actions in a crisis might leave a positive lasting image. No-one expects the world to run smoothly, and by keeping a clear head and displaying leadership as a crisis breaks, you can earn respect. Tony Blair's first few months in office have seen numerous examples of the Labour spin doctors turning stories round.

When the fuss over the donation from Bernie Eccleston to Labour was being stoked by the Tories, Blair announced a review of party funding as a whole. The Tories, who rely on secret donations, soon shut up. When a scandal broke over Glasgow MP Mohammed Sarwar's arrest, Blair used the chance to act as a tough leader. Compared to the last Tory term in office, when John Major lurched from one crisis to the next without time to recover, Blair's spin strategy worked.

Handling a Crisis Checklist

- ☑ Establish the facts, and quickly - you must know exactly what's going on.

- ☑ Establish a single authoritative source of information for journalists, and clamp down on all unauthorised sources of information.

- ☑ Be as honest and up-front as possible - do not stonewall or whitewash. Earn the trust of the journalists.

- ☑ Take responsibility for what has happened - do not blame others if it is your fault.

- ☑ Do something - the story must be moved on by your responses to the crisis.

- ☑ Turn it to your advantage - use the crisis to display concern, care, or strong leadership.

Rapid Rebuttal

R apid rebuttal is the technique used in political campaigns when spin doctors are engaged in hand-to-hand combat. It rests on the idea that no claim by the opposition should be allowed to be accepted as the truth. Even at the lowest levels of spin doctoring, the principle of rapid rebuttal applies.

For years the Labour Party would allow the Tories to tell all kinds of lies, and do nothing about it. The rationale was that by responding it gave them a dignity they didn't deserve, and that people wouldn't believe the nonsense put out by Conservative Central Office. Unfortunately, the strategy was flawed because people did believe the nonsense, and if you throw enough mud some of it sticks. Some say that a lie is halfway round the world before the truth is out the door.

By the 1997 General Election, senior Tories couldn't sneeze without Labour putting out a rebuttal. It was an awesome process to watch. No Tory speech, news conference or news release went unchecked. Within hours, sometimes within minutes, journalists would have something in their hands from Labour, putting their side of the argument, disputing the Tories' facts, and pointing out inconsistencies.

Labour's impressive rapid rebuttal was based on a computer database system called Excaliber, which logged thousands of articles, speeches, and news releases. If a Tory candidate said something on pensions, Labour's spin doctors had access within minutes to everything that person had ever said in public on pensions.

Of course, any database is only as good as the people using it. Many of the successes of Labour's rapid rebuttal were because of the humans operating the system, not the computer itself.

In August 1996, I was on both the receiving end and beneficial end of rapid rebuttal with just one story. I had published a Fabian Society pamphlet on modernising the monarchy, which these days seems pretty tame stuff given that the Queen's own thoughts on the subject are far more radical than mine. I was also, at the time, a Labour Party parliamentary candidate, and so when the story appeared on the front page of the *Times,* the Tories wheeled out Michael Portillo to accuse me of wanting to chop off the Royals' heads. The boys and girls at Millbank went to work.

Within minutes, Excaliber had identified a Conservative parliamentary candidate who had also written in support of modernising the monarchy, in even wackier terms. The article was three years old, and appeared in an obscure political journal, but it didn't matter. It was enough to shut the Tories up, and kill the story dead. Rapid rebuttal achieved success.

The lessons of Labour's rapid rebuttal operation for spin doctors everywhere is that nothing said by your opponents and rivals should ever be allowed to go unchallenged, without your own version of the truth being available. If a lie or distortion is allowed to be accepted, then people will assume it is true, no matter how absurd. That means someone else is shaping opinion about you, and you have lost control. Some of the lies that Labour failed to tackle in the early eighties (for example, that Labour councils banned black bin liners and the nursery rhyme 'Baa Baa Black Sheep) are still believed by some people. The lies have become accepted as fact.

Both Tories and Labour now use rapid rebuttal against one another. In March 1998, William Hague was accused by Labour of stealing key phrases from Tony Blair's conference speech and using them himself in a speech in Australia. The *Telegraph* ran a story on page two with the headline '*Hague accused of stealing Blair rhetoric*'. The Tory spin doctors didn't take the attack lying down. By the next day, the *Guardian* had a story 'Hague hits back at claims that he plagiarised Blair' with examples of speeches made by Blair which echoed John Major's speeches, plus, for good measure, things that Tony Blair had wished he never said, such as his 1983 demand for withdrawal from the EEC. The net result of all this rapid rebuttal was a no-score draw.

Rapid Rebuttal Checklist

☑ Never let a lie or distortion go unchallenged, no matter how ridiculous it may seem.

☑ Put your side of the argument, deploying facts and figures, quickly, before the lie can gain currency.

☑ Accuse your opponent of the same misdemeanour of which they are accusing you. They'll soon shut up if they know they are on thin ice.

Making Complaints

If you feel the coverage you have received in the media is unfair, you should complain. Part of the political spin doctors' job is to be on the phone for much of the day complaining - about perceived bias, lack of time given to an item, too much time given to an opponent, lack of prominence given to a story, an interview being dropped, or incorrect or slanted facts.

The process is on-going. It forms a central part of the continuous process of attrition between spinners and hacks. Some of the *machismo* associated with spin doctoring is the ability to pick up the phone to a respected journalist and attack their work, accuse them of sloppy journalism, threaten to complain to their editor, or freeze them out of the information loop. This bullying, aggressive, downright rude and abusive approach is contrasted with the flattering and charming cajolery which can be deployed when a journalist has done what you want.

The aim, ultimately, is to develop a degree of psychological dependence between the journalist and the spin doctor, so that they know if they're bad, they'll get told off, and if they're good, they'll get a pat on the back. The modern spin doctor takes his advice from a four-hundred year-old source. Machiavelli wrote in the *Prince* (1541) *'From this arises the following question: whether it is better to be loved than feared or the reverse. The answer is that one would like to be both the one and the other; but because it is difficult to combine them, it is far better to be feared than loved...'*

Occasionally the spin doctor is found out. Alastair Campbell was exposed complaining to BBC TV by fax that their news running order had the verdict in the OJ Simpson murder trial above Tony Blair's speech to 1995 Labour Party conference.

In December 1997, the *Today* programme leaked a letter from Labour's David Hill to the editor of the programme, Jon Barton. Hill, the party's chief media spokesman, had written to complain about an especially tough John Humphreys grilling of Harriet Harman. The story appeared on the front page of the *Guardian* (December 13th) with a full colour picture of Humphreys under the headline *'The man Labour wants to gag'*. Hill's letter is worth quoting:

'Dear John (sic), The John Humphreys problem has assumed new proportions after this morning's interview with Harriet Harman. In response, we have had a council of war and are now considering whether, as a party, we will suspend co-operation when you make bids through us for Government Ministers.

Individual Government departments will continue to make their own minds up, but we will now give very careful thought to any bid to us, in order to make sure that your listeners are not going to be subjected to a repeat of the ridiculous exchange this morning...John Humphreys interrupted so much that she (Harman) was never permitted to develop a single answer. No-one seeking to the find the Secretary of State's explanation would be any the wiser at the end of the 'interview'. Frankly, none of us feels that this can go on.'

Hill then suggests he and Barton *'talk, as this is now serious'*.

The leaked letter is an extreme example of the process which takes place day in day out. Complaining to editors, journalists, even owners, is part of the job. The leaked letter shows that spin doctors, as a last resort, can simply withdraw support from the news creation process - pick up their ball, and go home.

The skill of the spin doctor is knowing who to complain to: when to chastise the journalist responsible, and when to take the matter to their boss. In his incarnation as Labour's Head of Communications, Peter Mandelson's brilliant reputation stemmed from his understanding of the news creation process, and his knowledge of the individual journalists working in a particular newsroom on a particular day. Gordon Brown's spin doctor Charlie Wheelan is famed for his bluff dealings with journalists. If he thinks a story is bollocks, he will phone them up and say so. Sometimes it might be double bollocks, or even Euro-bollocks.

Everyone has the right to complain if you feel you have been misrepresented or unfairly treated. Complaining is a terribly un-British thing to do, and we don't like doing it, but the media can be guilty of terrible acts of unfairness and misrepresentation and they shouldn't be allowed to get away with it.

As Denis MacShane puts it in the seminal *Using the Media*: *'Complaining about **bad** media coverage is a vital part of the process of getting **good** media coverage.'*

If a story is incorrect, you should first of all phone the journalist responsible and point out the facts. If the journalist seems uninterested or hostile, phone up the duty editor. (Don't threaten to go to the editor of the *Times* or the Chairman of the BBC Governors - you'll look silly) It the dispute is over a matter of pure accuracy such as the wrong name put under a photograph or incorrect figures, the newspaper has a duty to print a correction in the next edition. These will appear as a small paragraphs at the bottom of a column, usually titled 'Correction'.

If your complaint rests on being misquoted, things are less simple. Journalists have the right to use part of what you say, to paraphrase what you say, and to put words into your mouth by asking you to agree with statements they put to you. Naturally, they'll use your quote to accentuate the angle they've taken with their story. A politician might say of a colleague *'He's a loveable old bastard, and we're the best of friends'*, but a journalist can report it as *'Cabinet rift over 'bastard' jibe'* You should try to keep records of exactly what you say - jot down notes as you talk to journalists, because they'll be doing the same thing. Bernard Ingham was famed for his rapid shorthand which meant he had verbatim notes of virtually every conversation he had. At the end of a conversation with a journalist ask them what quotes they've taken, and what they're going to use. You can try and correct them at this early stage if already they're going in an unfavourable direction. If your quote is made up, or gives a meaning entirely different from what you actually said, you have grounds to complain.

If your complaint is non-factual, and based on a sense of unfairness or distortion, you are on even shakier ground, but you should still complain. You might appeal to a sense of fairplay and natural justice, or to the news organisation's own producer guidelines, code of conduct, or even the National Union of Journalists code of conduct. This includes the stipulations that:

'A journalist shall strive to ensure that the information he/she disseminates is fair and accurate, avoids the expression of comment and conjecture as established fact,' and, 'a journalist shall rectify promptly any harmful inaccuracies, ensure that correction and apologies receive due prominence and afford the right to reply to persons criticised when the issue is of sufficient importance.'

Following the phone call, you should write a letter setting out your complaints. Marshal your case clearly and use rock solid facts. Copy the letter to the editor or producer. Your should try to secure some form of redress - either a printed correction or a guarantee that they will print a letter setting out your case on the *letters to the editor* page.

Such a letter can be a good way of setting the record straight (or at least straighter). Here's an example from Gez Segar, spin doctor for the Millennium Experience, in the *Sunday Telegraph* (28th December): *'Contrary to your front-page report, it is quite wrong to say that the Union flag will not feature in the Millennium Experience at Greenwich, etc.'* or this from Anne Fuller of the Magistrates Association in the *Sunday Times* on the same day: *'Contrary to Jonathan Leake's article, Magistrates Association's sentencing guidelines have been in use since April, etc.'*

If you cannot secure satisfaction from the culprits themselves (and most newspapers will accept the rap if they've genuinely got it wrong), you can take your complaint to an outside body. The Press Complaints Commission (0171 353 1248) covers all newspapers and magazines. The Broadcasting Complaints Commission (0171 630 1966) covers television. The BBC Complaints Unit (0171 580 4468) can take complaints about the BBC's output. In the commercial sector the Independent Television Commission (0171 255 3000) and the Radio Authority (0171 430 2724) cover independent TV and radio.

Complaints checklist

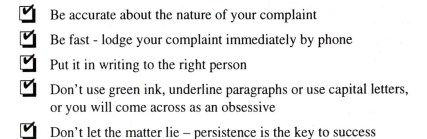

☑ Be accurate about the nature of your complaint

☑ Be fast - lodge your complaint immediately by phone

☑ Put it in writing to the right person

☑ Don't use green ink, underline paragraphs or use capital letters, or you will come across as an obsessive

☑ Don't let the matter lie – persistence is the key to success

Spin Doctoring and the Law

A lthough some spin doctors behave as though they are above the law, and some are a law unto themselves, they must operate within the same legal framework as everyone else in the media. The law in Britain does not treat journalists, spin doctors, newspaper editors or owners differently from anybody else.

Whilst censorship was abolished in most circumstances in the 1690's, spin doctors do not enjoy absolute freedom of speech; they are covered by laws stemming from custom, statute and precedent. Britain's recent incorporation of the European Convention on Human Rights into domestic law enshrines article ten which says, *'Everyone has the right to freedom of expression. This shall include freedom to hold opinions and to receive or impart information and ideas without interference by public authority'*. Any restrictions on this right must be justified as 'necessary in a democratic society.'

The law of defamation is one of the most important laws to be acutely aware of - it could be very costly if you don't. The law defines a defamatory statement as one which damages a person's reputation by exposing them to hatred, contempt, shame, or ridicule or makes them likely to be shunned or avoided. Defamation covers attacking a person's honour, injuring a person or company in following their business, or to wrongly accuse them of criminal activity, dishonesty, hypocrisy, incompetence, cruelty, inefficiency, or stupidity. If the defamation is written it is called libel, if spoken, it is slander.

If accused of defamation the first step is to do what our American friends describe as 'lawyering-up'. Names and addresses of legal firms can be gleaned from a reference work called the Legal 500. There are many legal firms such as Clifford Chance, Hempsons, Frere Cholmeley Bischoff, Mishcon de Reya, Richards Butler, and most famously Peter Carter-Ruck and Partners which list defamation as a specialism. You can even get libel insurance, but the premiums are high. There are defences against charges of defamation, but the best bet is to consult a lawyer.

There are also codes of conduct which should influence the spin doctor, not least the Institute of Public Relations Code of Professional Conduct which holds members to have *'regard for the public interest'*, *'respect the truth'*, *'not disseminate false or misleading information'* and *'honour confidences'*.

Spin doctoring and the law checklist

☑ Gain an understanding the laws of slander and libel, and tread extremely carefully.

☑ Take legal advice if you're are unsure.

The Really Dirty Stuff

To be honest, there are occasions when spin doctors do things that might seem to the casual observer distasteful. I'm not defending amoral or illegal behaviour, but no book on spin doctoring should ignore some of the really dirty stuff that goes on.

Leaks

This is a time-honoured method of getting confidential or restricted information into the hands of journalists. By its very nature 'leaking' implies that the information has news value: if someone somewhere doesn't want the information released, there must be a good reason why. The technique is simple enough. Just slip a journalist the material to be leaked in a brown envelope over lunch, or even post it after a phone-call tipping them off. In the House of Commons the traditional method is to 'leave it on the photo-copier' for someone to find. Journalists are honour-bound never to reveal their sources, so if you're caught, it won't be their fault.

Leaks can be used to 'fly a kite' – to see how public opinion reacts to a particular proposal or idea. If the response is rioting in the streets, the proposal can be disowned.

They can also be used to steer a public debate in a certain direction. A leak to the *Today* programme of a 'confidential internal MOD report' showing that without extra Government funding, the Royal Navy will have no ships by the year 2010 is a good way of winning support for defence expenditure.

The Buckingham Palace spin doctors (spin doctors by appointment?) flew a kite in November 1997 when they tipped journalists off about a plan to open Kensington Palace to the public. They wanted to give the impression of 'modernisation' while also gauging opinion, without having to do anything or make any commitments. Later that year, they tried the same thing with a story about dropping the Imperial titles from the Honours system. In 1998 they started against by suggesting the number of 'HRHs' will be reduced. These leaks create the illusion of change and fresh thinking, in tune with popular opinion, and can be denied later if necessary.

In politics, everything leaks like a sieve. Indèed, as Sir Humphrey puts it in *Yes Minister*, *'The ship of state is the only ship that leaks from the top.'* The difference between leaking and briefing is best elucidated by former Prime Minister James Callaghan: *'You know the difference between leaking and briefing: leaking is what you do, briefing is what I do.'*

A good example of the political leak is the news which appeared in December 1997 that Cabinet Minister David Blunkett was furious with the handling of the Labour Government's welfare reforms, and was leading the charge to prevent cuts in disabled persons allowances. Blunkett was portrayed as a heroic defender of the poor, in a morass of nasty, mean Cabinet Ministers. The newspapers found this out because of the leak of a letter between Blunkett and Chancellor Gordon Brown. I wonder how that happened? David Blunkett was reported to be furious at the leak, according to his spin doctor Conor Ryan, and of course strenuously denied any suggestion that the leak came from him.

In the lead-up to the 1998 Budget, the Treasury sprung more leaks than the Titanic. The papers in the weeks leading up to the Chancellors announcements were filled with leaked snippets of information. The Sunday newspapers before the Budget included headlines such as 'Brown plans to abolish deficit' (*Sunday Times*), 'Museum charges to be scrapped' (*Independent on Sunday*) and 'Brown to tax middle-class child benefit' (*Sunday Times*). The 1998 Budget was subject to the most spin in British political history.

Leaks can backfire. When someone leaked advance details of Kenneth Clarke's 1996 Budget and they found their way via freelance Peter Hounam to the *Mirror*, the editor Piers Morgan gave it back. Perhaps he decided there was more novelty value in a tabloid editor doing the decent thing rather than simply splashing the leak all over page one.

Be warned. Some organisations employ counter-leaking methods. One way is for each copy of a document to contain an imperceptible and unique form of words or punctuation, so that a stack of what seems like the same document can each be sourced to the recipient.

The stakes can be high if you are caught. In September 1983 a civil servant in the Foreign Office, Sarah Tisdall, was jailed for six months for leaking information about the deployment of Cruise Missiles in Britain. Another civil servant, Clive Ponting was tried at the Old Bailey for leaking details of the sinking of the Belgrano.

Spin doctors can use the convention of leaking to their advantage. Releasing unpromising material with the added glamour of confidentiality, and making the journalist on the receiving end feel like Woodward or Bernstein, may improve the chances of a hit. The journalist will never know whether the story was genuinely confidential, or destined for release anyway.

Briefing against your enemies

When things turn nasty, spin doctors have to brief the media against their enemies - who should never be confused with opponents. Your opponents are those in rival firms, teams, organisations or parties who are just doing their job in trying to get you. Enemies are the ones who claim to be your friends. Your enemies are usually 'within'.

The established spin doctor can use his or her trusted relationship with a journalist to do their enemy down: so-and-so is destined for the chop, so-and-so is weak and spineless. It was a spin doctor, using the non-

attributable briefing as cover, who described Bill Morris in a newspaper as '*pusillanimous*', and another who described John Biffin as a '*semi-detached member of the Government*'. Biffen later described Bernard Ingham (for it was he) as the 'sewer and not the sewage' for that particular piece of spin doctoring.

Briefing against your enemies doesn't have to be vicious - it can be a case of spreading strange rumours or placing negative images into peoples' heads.

There is a rumour doing the rounds that a certain MP has been caught not wearing any knickers in the House of Commons. The story appeared on the front page of the *Sunday Times* on 28th December as a news item, filled with innuendo and *Carry On* style puns. The headline was '*Whips are out for the bare-bottomed Blair babe*', and the intro was '*The barefaced cheek of the act is the talk of the parliamentary tearooms.*' The MP in question does herself no favours by reportedly stating that she wants, '*to get to the bottom of where all this is coming from.*'

Alastair Campbell, when working for *Today* newspaper, claimed credit for the image of John Major tucking his shirt into his underpants. The image was taken a step further by Steve Bell's cartoons in the *Guardian* which had Major wearing his pants on the outside of his trousers - a sort of anti-superman.

John Major's spin doctor Sheila Gunn has claimed responsibility for starting the rumour that Cherie Booth, wife of the PM Tony Blair, had it in for Humphrey the Downing Street cat. When Humphrey went missing from Downing Street, newspapers speculated that Cherie Booth, in a display of Cruella De Ville tendencies, had instructed the wretched feline to be put down. Sheila Gunn told the *Times* '*it was just one of those ideas that came into my head. It wasn't based on any justification.*' (Humphrey, in case you were worried, is at the time of writing alive and well.)

Misinformation

This really belongs to the world of espionage and conspiracy theory, rather than spin doctoring. The spin doctor is finished if caught deliberately lying to journalists. You can tell some of the truth, even leave information out of the discussion, but to tell a straight-forward lie is professional suicide. Black propaganda is the stuff of the KGB and CIA.

Perhaps the most famous example of misinformation is the Zinoviev Letter. The Zinoviev Letter was the (probably forged by the British Secret Service) invitation in 1924 from the Soviet leadership to the British working class to start a revolution. It appeared on the front pages of the right-wing newspapers in the week of the August 1924 General Election, and undoubtedly cost the Labour Party votes. The reds-under-the-beds scare story was still working even after the fall of Communism. In the 1992 General Election, the *Sunday Times* ran a front-page story claiming to have unearthed 'Kinnock's Kremlin Connection'. The 'connection' rested on the discovery of a KGB file on Kinnock - no great surprise as the KGB had files on all the leaders in western democracies including Margaret Thatcher and Ronald Regan.

Peter Wright's revelations in '*Spycatcher*' showed that a group of intelligence officers sought to malign politicians by starting rumours and spreading misinformation with journalists. This included the ludicrous suggestion that Harold Wilson and Edward Heath were Soviet agents, various government ministers were communists, and that Labour leader Hugh Gaitskell was murdered by the KGB. In the lead-up to the 1974 General Election Peter Wright claims that '*MI5 would arrange for selective details of the intelligence about leading Labour Party figures, but especially Wilson, to be leaked to sympathetic pressmen. Using our contacts in the press and among union officials, word of the material contained in the MI5 files and the fact that Wilson was considered a security risk would be passed around.*'

Journalist Paul Foot claims that during the 1970's journalists were often recipients of phone-calls from 'freelance journalists' offering photographic evidence of a very senior politician's impropriety. The photos didn't exist, but the Fleet Street gossip machine would soon spread the smear.

Indeed there are a number of malicious rumours doing the rounds about senior figures at any given moment. Current ones concern the sexuality of prominent politicians, inside and outside the House of Commons; a story about a famous journalist, a new MP, and a coffee table; and endless tales of drug addiction, alcoholism and sexual impropriety. They do the rounds in the pubs and restaurants of Westminster, reappear in different forms and about different people. Not even MPs can have that much fun for all the rumours to be true.

Turning the Rumour Mill

Less damaging than outright misinformation is releasing information about yourself so that you get talked about.

Every organisation or social circle has a person who everyone knows is the purveyor of quality gossip. These people set themselves up as the trading post in rumours. They can be used, like any other media. In the House of Commons, reputations can be made or broken by a whip placing a tip-off here or a word in the right ear there, and letting the gossips in the tea-room, Sports and Social Club and Members Bars go to work. In companies, people assemble in the canteen, in the smokers' room (or outside), by the coffee machine, and what was told in confidence at 9am will be common currency by 5pm.

A master of turning the rumour mill is spin doctor, columnist and author Derek Draper. In the decade I have known Derek Draper, from when we were both Labour student activists in Manchester, he has been at the centre of attention in whatever circles he has moved. From the student union, to Number Ten, Derek has ensured that people always knew what schemes he was up to. Sometimes the gossip about him is absurd and scurrilous, sometimes alarmingly accurate. These days, the rumour mill is fuelled by newspaper diaries, but wherever two or three are gathered who know him, the conversation will inevitably turn to his latest exploits. He skilfully nurtures his own image, and is successful as a result.

Derek Draper is already rich. I confidently predict he will be an international celebrity or leading politician by the time he is forty.

Try starting a rumour in your organisation, and see how long it takes to come back to you. Tell someone in confidence that you're being headhunted by a rival firm, or that the boss has got you working on a top-secret project, or that you've been asked to draw up a list of colleagues to be promoted or sacked. Then stand back and watch the results.

Spoilers

A spoiler is the device used by rival journalists or spin doctors to undermine, detract or divert attention from a news story. Journalists use it to distract attention from a rival's exclusive story. They either come up with a rival scoop, or simply steal the story and run it themselves. This is possible because first editions of newspapers' front pages are available the afternoon or evening before publication. In central London, you can buy first editions of 'tomorrow's papers' from about 11pm onwards. Newspapers, especially the tabloids, can see what their rivals have done, and spoil it, try to find a new angle, or simply steal it. There is a rumour that a resourceful journalist on a tabloid hacked into the computer system of the rival tabloid and stole the front page.

Spin doctors use a spoiler to distract attention from a damaging story about themselves or their masters. The story about then-Labour Leader Neil Kinnock being on KGB files. (The implication being that he must somehow be a Soviet 'agent of influence') was dealt with by Labour using a spoiler. As soon as David Hill, Labour's spin doctor-in-chief was tipped off about *the Sunday Times's* intentions to run the spurious 'exclusive' as a front page lead 'Kinnock's Kremlin Connection', he didn't try and persuade them to stop it. He spent his Saturday night phoning all the *Sunday Times's* rival papers giving them the story. Thus he destroyed the *Sunday Times's* hopes of an exclusive and the impact of the story, and ensured that the other papers carried the story with plenty of Labour spin.

During the 1997 Labour Party conference, Peter Mandelson came in for some media flak for remarks he made during a fringe meeting on the minimum wage. As soon as the media pack came hunting for Mandelson, a new, much better story emerged which set them running after a new quarry. An audio-tape of Tony Banks describing William Hague as 'a foetus' at the Tribune Rally suddenly came to light forty-eight hours after he made the remarks, and the media began 'Banks gaffes again – should he be sacked?' story. The Mandelson remarks were forgotten. A cynical person might suggest the two events were not entirely unconnected, although I have it on excellent authority that they were not connected in any way.

The *Daily Telegraph* in February 1998 accused Labour of deliberately floating two 'entirely bogus stories' (about saving the Royal Yacht and Chris Patten being investigated for leaking government documents) to deflect media attention away from the semi-scandal of Robin Cook's divorce. A good spin doctor will always have a good spoiler up their sleeve.

Bribery

There is a growing and unethical form of bribery in journalism which involves linking the publication of editorial material to the placing of advertisements. In other words unscrupulous publications will use your news release, as long as your organisation pays for an advert in the same publication. The coverage is conditional on the payment. This tends to be practised by smaller magazines and local papers. This should be resisted. If I'm ever offered such a deal, I report them to the NUJ.

Another scam is the use of charges for colour separations on photographs. This means the publication will use your photograph, but charge you for the privilege. These forms of bribery damage the relationship between spin doctors and journalists, reducing it to one of simple buying and selling, and also undermines decent standards of journalism.

However, rest assured that large-scale bribery plays no part in spin doctoring. The spin doctor never need resort to such obvious and disreputable tactics, because as the famous words of Humbert Wolfe rightly tell us:

> *'You cannot hope to bribe or twist*
> *thank God the British journalist.*
> *But seeing what the man will do*
> *unbribed, there's no occasion to.'*

Conclusion

What is the future for spin doctoring? As the media transforms into a multi-channel, multi-publication 24-hour leviathan, the role and opportunities for spin doctors will increase. In the early part of the next century, no politician, business leader, star or celeb will be without their own personal spin doctor. In Britain, the business of spin doctoring will increasingly mirror that of the United States, with the best spin doctors acting as hired guns for the biggest payers or most-likely-to-succeed politicians. The spin doctor of the future will rely on new types of media and communication as alien to us as the Internet would be to Gladstone or Disraeli. Just as journalists learn new ways of reporting events, so spin doctors will learn new ways of spinning.

A second prediction is that spin doctors will be further dragged from the dark shadows and into the limelight. It can't be long before the biographies of Whelan and Campbell are vying for space in book-shops alongside the biographies of their political masters.

This is no bad thing. The more transparent and open the process of news creation becomes, the better it is for democracy. The more the Old Boys' Networks can be unravelled, the better. The clearer we understand where and how the news we read, watch and listen to, has come from, the better informed we will become.

In the future, I hope that no one reads a newspaper or watches a news bulletin in a state of passivity. All citizens should understand that news comes from certain processes, and is not dished out as a result of unseen forces. We should be constantly questioning the media, asking who's pulling the strings and why. The more people have access to the media, can make themselves heard, can complain when things go wrong, and can stop journalists stitching them up, the better media we will have.

I hope this book has proved useful. I have tried to divulge all the tricks of the trade I know from a decade in the business, and show how the spin doctors in politics and business work to mould the media around us.

But remember – **anyone can be a spin doctor**. Write a letter to the paper, dial up a phone-in, try drafting a news release for the local paper. There are plenty of good causes which do not get the profile they deserve, not because their arguments are weak, but because of a lack of good spin doctoring.

Start now. Don't let other people shape the media – have a go yourself. Go on, be your own spin doctor.

Appendix One

Spot The Spin

If you doubt the importance of spin doctoring in the modern communications age, then I invite you to play 'spot the spin.' The aim of the game is simple enough: to identify what proportion of the 'news' has been tracked down by Woodward and Bernstein-style investigative journalists, and what proportion has been influenced by spin doctors.

Take a selection of the daily papers, and a marker pen, and highlight anything with a spin doctor's grubby fingerprints all over it. It's a disillusioning process for anyone who thought news was produced by resourceful hacks in dogged pursuit of the truth.

A look at some national newspapers reveals the extent of the spin doctors' influence.

The *Sun* (28th November 1997) has a full page story on page six about Britain's most wanted on-the-run criminals. Ten villain's grim mugshots and criminal CV's are listed. Is this an example of investigative journalism in the public interest? When you read the story, its a plug for the new ITV series '*Most Wanted*' with Penny Smith and Dermot Murnaghan. The idea, information, and photographs have all been supplied by the makers of the programme, via their spin doctors.

The *Times* (27th December) has the lead story '*Cook may quit the Cabinet to run as Scots PM*' '*Senior aides*' told Philip Webster that Robin Cook is '*seriously considering the matter.*' How does Webster know the inner workings of the Foreign Secretary's mind? Because a spin doctor told him. (A few weeks later, Cook hit the headlines again with a story stating that he had ruled out running as Scots PM - a second bite at the media cherry for very little effort). The *Observer* (30th November 1997) claims '*Cabinet draws up plans to save pit jobs*'. The writer of the story Patrick Wintour wasn't at the Cabinet Committee which drew up the plans, and the plans haven't been published, so how does he know? Because a spin doctor told him.

The charity Age Concern scored a big hit with this story in the *Observer* (15th March 1998): *'Don't make me beg for a decent wage'*. The focuses on the plight of pensioner Angela Sinclair, 77, who despite being in the top-earning bracket for pensioners, has to live on £150 per week. The peg for the story is Age Concern's report *Raising the Age of Retirement* which came out the following day. The Age Concern spin doctors have done everything right. They have trailed their report in advance of publication by letting a Sunday paper run an exclusive, and they have backed it up with a 'real person' case study, and their reward for successful spinning is a big piece in a respected national newspaper.

In the *Observer* (30th November 1997) there's a good example of commercial spin: *'Airship reborn as green jam-buster'* is the headline on a story about the launching of a fleet of airships called 'Cargolifters' as environmentally-sustainable alternatives to rail or road. The story lists every dimension and statistic of the new craft, alongside a raft of the German company chairman's quotes - all supplied to journalists by the firm's *spinnen doktors*. The article - as near to free advertising as you can get - is the stuff of spin doctors' dreams.

The manufacturers of Lava Lamps, Mathmos, scored a direct hit with their story about a pre-Christmas rush on their product. The *Evening Standard* on Christmas eve 1997 ran a short news story *'Shoppers turn on to Lava lamps'* alongside a photograph of the product, and a quote from Mathmos saying they'd been working round the clock to meet demand.

Two more examples of commercial spin: 'GIs play war with our clockwork toys' is a story on the front page of the *Observer* (15th March 1998) which claims the US army has commissioned the inventor of the clockwork radio to create clockwork weapons systems. The story has been placed there by BayGen, the company which has been commissioned. The article is by-lined Marie Woolf, consumer affairs correspondent, who presumably was as pleased to be on the front page as BayGen were. 'Titanic tax haven to sail with 65,000' appears in the *Sunday Times* (15th March 1998). The story concerns plans for a giant floating Millionaires paradise. As one reads the story, it becomes clear that the 'floating Monaco' is still on the drawing-board of the engineering company Engineering Solutions.

That's just the news pages. The business pages, entertainment pages, TV pages and sports pages are equally prone to the spin doctors' guile.

The *Guardian's* business pages (13th December 1997) carry *'Burton in mail order venture'*, *'Direct Line in pension assault'*, and *'South West Expands'*. Full marks to the spin doctors of Burton Group, Direct Line Insurance, and South West Water for securing good news stories about their companies. The personal finance section of the *Sun* on December 18 leads with *'Bank sets standard'* - a story about a new phone bank account launched by Standard Life, complete with photo of the boss.

In any selection of newspapers it is the same. Some stories will have been originated by an organisation's press office team, and given to journalists. Some stories will concern the great and the good, and be filled with facts, interpretation, and quotes given by their spin doctors. Commercial PR agencies will have placed stories about their clients' products. Celebrities' spokespeople will have placed stories in the gossip and entertainment section. The Letters Page and Diary column will betray the influence of the media manipulators. No part of the newspaper, from news to features, to sports and letters, is free of spin.

The influence of the hidden spin doctor extends into radio and television. Listen to the stories which appear on the radio news. How many are about new reports or surveys? Watch the television news. How much of it is taken up with cleverly contrived photo-opportunities and sound-bites?

The media is under constant attack from those who want to use and abuse it. The influence of the spin doctors is huge - next time you reach for your morning paper or turn on the TV or radio, try and spot the spin. I warn you: you will never look at a newspaper or watch television news in the same way again.

Appendix Two

Hits, Misses and Maybe's

A ll journalists receive hundreds of news releases. Here's a small selection sent to the news desk of the *Bradford Telegraph and Argus*, and reporter Lorraine Eames's judgement of them.

❶ The first is from the Imperial Cancer Research Fund.
The headline is: *'Get your church to plant a rose bush for Mother's Day and Help the Imperial Cancer Research Fund.'*
And the intro reads: *'Mothering Sunday will soon be here and the Imperial Cancer Research Fund is urging church-goers to join forces to support its Mothering Sunday Rose Appeal and help raise money for the charity's vital £53 million a year research programme.'*
Lorraine says: *'We might follow this up for picture, but only if a church in our area took part in the appeal'*. This one's a maybe.

❷ The West Yorkshire Police press office have issued this release
'Making the Most of Neighbourhood watch'
'A brand new approach is being taken to Neighbourhood Watch as Eccleshill members get together for their annual conference.'
Lorraine says this is the most likely to score a hit: *'We'll probably cover this - its a specific area and a specific event which might be newsworthy. We'll possibly publish something beforehand, and send someone to the meeting.'* A hit!

❸ The next is from the Gas Consumers Council.
'GCC consumer representations'
'Today, the Gas Consumers Council (GCC) issues its figures for consumer representations during 1997. The council dealt with 273,895 representations, of which 44,482 were category A complaints.'
Lorraine's comment is *'too long and not specific enough to Bradford. I might phone to find any anecdotal information for our area.'* Another maybe.

❹ The fourth, issued by a PR company who ought to know better, is a release about the Guardian Direct Cup, a tennis championship.
'Rusedski christens Battersea Park site'.
Lorraine's reaction, *'Completely irrelevant to Bradford'*. A miss.

❺ Lastly, a release from Yorkshire and Humberside Development Agency.
'English Partnerships Secondee for YHDA'
'English Partnerships have extended their support for the region's effort to win inward investment by seconding a member of staff to Yorkshire and Humberside Development Agency.'
Lorraine sums it up: *'Boring, and not geared towards a specific area or district.'* A miss.

Appendix Three

A Model News Release

At the top goes your organisation's name and logo

NEWS RELEASE

FOR IMMEDIATE RELEASE: 20th April 1998 (or EMBARGO: 00.01hrs 21st April 1998)
For attention of Newsdesks
Contact: Your name here, and 24 hour contact numbers

THE HEADLINE SHOULD BE SHORT AND SNAPPY

THE FIRST PARAGRAPH is where you make your impact. Here you must have the guts of the story. Use the Five-W formula, and ensure that the most newsworthy angle is up front. Think of hard news, not fluff or conjecture. Remember you only have seconds to win the journalist over

If you are lucky, the journalist has read on to the second paragraph. Here's your change to expand on some of the details in the first paragraph, and go a little deeper into the Five-Ws.

Extra paragraphs should never 'bury' any new information, but seek to expand on aspects of the information presented above.

Near the end, you can add a quote. *'This might be italicised, and be snappy and crisp, without being over-the-top.'* You need to add the name and position of the spokesperson.

ends (if the copy has come to an end, write 'ends')
more follows (if you are continuing onto another sheet, write 'more follows')

NOTES TO EDITORS

1) The first Note to Editors explains who you are and what you stand for.
2) Other notes can provide background information and context, or alert the journalist to a interview opportunity or the availability of a document or briefing paper.

FOR MORE INFORMATION CONTACT: Your name and numbers.

Further Reading

There are plenty of books on the media, journalism, public relations and political communications (but none on the techniques of spin doctoring until now!) Most of the PR textbooks are a little dull, and often the text book advice doesn't match up to real experience. I've included a selection of the best ones here. I've also thrown in a biography of spin doctor Bernard Ingham which sheds a little light on the trade. The biography most people are waiting for - that of Peter Mandelson – is planned for 1998.

All About Public Relations Roger Haywood (McGraw Hill second ed, 1991)

English for Journalists Wynford Hicks (Routledge 1993)

From Soapbox to Soundbite – party political campaigning in Britain since 1945 Martin Rosenbaum (Macmillian 1997)

Good and Faithful Servant - the Unauthorised Biography of Bernard Ingham Robert Harris (Faber and Faber 1990)

Guardian Media Guide eds. Steve Peak and Paul Fisher (Forth Estate 1998)

News and Journalism in the UK Brian McNair (Routledge 1984)

Practical Media Relations Judith Ridgway (Gower 1984)

Public Relations Frank Jefkins (Pitman Publishing 1992)

PR! A Social History of Spin Stuart Ewen (Basic Books 1996)

Quick and Dirty Guide to PR (IPR Local Government Group 1997)

Sources Close to the Prime Minister – inside the hidden world of the news manipulators Michael Cockerell, Peter Hennessy and David Walker (MacMillan 1984)

Spin Doctors and Soundbites Nicholas Jones (Cassell 1995)

Spin Control John Anthony Maltese (University of North Carolina Press 1994)

Teach Yourself Journalism Michael Bromley (Hodder and Stoughton 1994)

The Newspapers Handbook Richard Keeble (Routledge 1994)

The Radio Handbook Pete Wilby and Andy Conroy (Routledge 1994)

Using the Media Denis MacShane (Pluto 1979)

Glossary of Spin Doctoring Terms

Actuality sound of an event or an interviewee used on radio.

Advertorial a paid-for advertisement masquerading as a genuine article in a newspaper. Advertorials are frowned upon by the Institute of Public Relations and the National Union of Journalists, but if you've got the budget, don't let that put you off.

Angle the aspect of a story which you chose to stress, usually one of the **five W's (qv)**. Also known as 'peg' (the thing on which the story hangs).

Aston the description that appears on the TV screen of a spokesperson or interviewee on TV under their name, designed to let viewers know who you are. eg 'Prime Minister', 'Church of England' or ' 'anti-hunt campaigner'. Named after the Aston machine which makes the words appear.

Background part of an article which supplies information to place the story in context.

Banner headline on the front page of a newspaper which extends across the full page.

Broadsheet large size newspaper such as the *Times* or *Guardian.*

Body text the main bulk of the text in a newspaper or magazine article, excluding **headlines (qv)**, **standfirsts, (qv)** or **by-lines (qv)**.

Bulletin news programme (UK) or news item (USA).

By-line the name of the journalist who has written the piece when it appears above their article. The by-line '*By Our Correspondent*' usually means the **copy (qv)** has come from an agency.

Catchline the single word used at the top of a news release or copy in a newsroom used to identify the story.

Clip a short piece of sound recorded for radio or TV.

Clippings see cuttings.

Caption words describing photograph or graphic in a publication, or on the back of a photograph sent to publications.

Cans jargon for headphones in radio stations.

Case study what journalists love – real people. A case study is a real example of a person or group of people describing their experiences, and available for journalists to use.

Columnist journalist (often highly paid) who writes a personal column for publication, setting out their view of current events, what they've been up to that week, which parties they went to, and so on.

Conference the morning meeting of newsroom staff on a publication or broadcasters to discuss stories for that day's running order or edition of daily newspaper.

Contact person with useful information or services. For the spin doctor the most useful contacts tend to be journalists (and vice versa).

Copy written material for publication. Can be editorial copy (news and features) or advertising copy (the text which appears on ads).

Copy flow the route which **copy (qv)** takes within a news organisation, usually from reporter to sub to section editor to editor. A good spin doctor understands the copy flow within an organisation in order to be able to have influence at different levels.

Crop to cut a photograph to make it fit the space in a publication, or to create a particular effect.

Cub a trainee reporter.

Cuts/Cuttings the library held by news organisations of articles cut from newspapers, stored by person or subject.

Crosshead small heading used to break up a column of text, usually centred.

Diary piece news based on timetabled predictable sources such as news conferences, debates in the House of Commons, business results, football matches, etc.

Diary humorous, gossipy, trivial column appearing in most newspapers and magazines, filled with tales of the embarrassments and misdemeanours of the great and the good. Usually appears under a nom de plume.

Down-spin to play down the importance of a (usually damaging) event or statement. *'That's not important; this really isn't a story...'* See **up-spin**.

Down-table subs See sub-editor.

ends the word that appears at the end of the copy in a news release, to let the journalist know the copy has finished.

Editorial the column in a newspaper which expresses its own opinion on a matter of importance. Also: all copy in a newspaper that is not advertising material.

Embargo the time stipulated on a news release before which information cannot be used.

Exclusive story given to one news outlet to the exclusion of all the others. Useful tool of spin doctoring, as this creates leverage over how the story is run, and earns credits with the journalist you give it to.

Feature longer article (as distinct from news) which covers an issue in greater depth, with more detail and colour, and less constrained by the conventions of news reporting.

Filler a short article used to fill up space in a publication.

Five W's the components of a story: who, what, where, why and when.

Freebie description of any trip, visit, meal or gift given for nothing, usually to journalists in the hope of favourable coverage or favours.

Freelance self-employed journalist.

Freesheet newspaper distributed to readers free.

Hack jocular and slightly derisory word for journalist. Can also be applied to student politicians.

House-style set of rules applied to the writing of a publication or organisation, covering capitals or lower case, captions, dates, numbers, etc.

Ghost-writer one employed to write articles, letters, even books in the name of another person.

Kill when an editor decides not to use your article. 'Kill fee' is the contractual agreement to pay a contributor a fee even if the article doesn't appear. Also describes what you want to do to the editor after they've dropped your piece.

Lead-time the amount of time ahead of publication that a newspaper or magazine needs material by. On major glossy magazines, the lead-time can be months.

Leak the unauthorised release of confidential material to the media (or the pretence of doing so, orchestrated by a spin doctor).

Literal spelling or typographical mistake as it appears in written copy. Also: **typo**.

news agency news-gathering organisation which sells its news and information to print and broadcast media. National and international agencies serve newsrooms via a on-line link-up, still known as a **'wire' (qv)**. (as in *'what's running on the wires?'*

news desk the front-line in a news operation, where news, information and tip-offs are first received by reporters and news stories are written.

News conference event where journalists given information from an organisation or individual. Usually only used for high-profile news stories.

News release the short document posted or faxed to journalists by spin-doctors to entice them into covering your story. Most news releases end up in the bin within seconds of receipt. As well as news, can cover operational information and notice of events like news **conferences (qv)** and **photo-opportunities (qv)**.

NIB acronym for News In Brief – the short 30-40 word items of news which appear in columns in newspapers.

Masthead the title of a newspaper or magazine as on the front page.

mf (more follows). The signal at the bottom right-hand side of a news release that another page follows on.

Package a broadcast report made of different components: interview, comment, or music.

Panel the sections of text pulled out of an article (usually attention-grabbing phrases) and placed between two lines, used to break up long articles.

Par journalists shorthand for paragraph. Sometimes **para**.

Patch the geographical area covered by a local newspaper or the area covered by a particular journalist.

Photo-opportunities staged events designed to provide newspapers with good photographs.

Pre-recorded term denoting that a radio or television interview is taped in advance of broadcast, and can be subject to editing.

Press Officer Old-fashioned term for **PRO (qv)**. Can refer to senior figures. Alistair Campbell is described as 'Tony Blair's Press Officer'.

PRO Public relations officer (or 'press relations officer'). Junior spin-doctor employed by organisation to draft and issue news releases, field calls from journalists, etc.

Press release see news release.

puff over the top sucking-up to an editor, client, product manufacturer or your boss in an article or news release. Also: **puffery, puff-piece.**

Off-message when a spokesman veers away from the agreed position or line during an interview or conversation with a journalist. Staying in control of the information you give to the media is called being **on-message.**

On spec when you send an article to the media without prior agreement for publication, in the, usually vain, hope that it will be used.

Op ed the page in a newspaper opposite the editorial, usually used for longer **think pieces (qv)** and opinion features. The prime spot for your article to appear.

Screamer slang for exclamation mark.

Silly season the period each year around August when most people are on holiday, and therefore there's little hard news. This can be the spin-doctors most fruitful time, because newsrooms are desperate for material.

Sign-off the name of the journalist who has written the article, when it appears at the end of the text. See also **by-line (qv).**

Sound-bite the short, snappy phrase used to make a point on radio or TV, usually under 20 seconds long, e.g. *'tough on crime, tough on the causes of crime'.*

Spin control the influence on the process of news creation exercised by spin doctors.

Spin doctor if you don't know by now…

Splash the lead story on the front page of a newspaper.

Spoiler a news story used by a newspaper to undermine, detract or attract attention away from a rival's story.

Standfirst the text between the headline and the main text, often used on features and longer news pieces, to draw the reader into the article.

Sub-editor (sub) print journalist who checks and edits spelling, grammar, **house-style (qv),** and length of articles, writes captions for photographs, **panels (qv) standfirsts (qv)** and lays out the page. The sub-editor in charge is called the 'chief sub' and the sub-editor charged with giving the page a final check is the 'stone sub'. The rest of the sub-editors are called 'down-table subs'.

Up-spin to accentuate the importance of a seemingly unimportant event or statement.

Vox pop 'voice of the people' interview conducted with members of the public, usually conducted in the street on a particular subject.

wire news agency (Press Association, Reuters, or Associated Press) which transmits stories and photographs via computers straight into newsrooms.

WOB headline reversed out of a black background.

Working-head headline used to remind everyone what the story is about.

About The Author

PAUL RICHARDS is senior public relations counsellor at Chelgate Ltd. He has worked in media relations for the London Borough of Barnet, English Partnerships, the Association of County Councils, the Royal National Institute for Deaf People, and the Labour Party. He was winner of the Advertising Standards Authority and Incorporated Society of British Advertisers awards for excellence in the 1996 Communications Advertising and Marketing examinations.

Paul Richards was Labour's parliamentary candidate at Billericay in the 1997 General Election. He is author of *'Long to Reign Over Us?'*, the Fabian Society study into the future of the Monarchy. He has appeared on *Newsnight, Today, Wogan* and radio and TV in USA, Japan, China, and throughout Europe, and has written for the *Guardian, New Statesman, Tribune*, and *Punch*. He is a member of the National Union of Journalists, the Society of Authors and the English Speaking Union.

Paul Richards lives in Hammersmith, West London. You can contact him through Take That Ltd., PO Box 200, Harrogate HG1 2YR.

Paul's next book will be *Spinning on the Net: A Practical Guide To Spin Doctoring On The Internet*

A LIST OF MEDIA CONTACTS (National Dailys, National Sundays, Regional Dailys, Radio, Television, and News Agencies) on self-adhesive labels can be obtained from Take That Ltd. For details, please email sales@takethat.co.uk or 'phone 01423-507545.

Take That Ltd. books are available at special quantity discounts to use as premiums and sales promotions, or for use in corporate training programs. For more information, please contact the Director of Special Sales at the above address or contact your local bookshop.